Creating Adaptable Teams

Creating Adaptable Teams

From the Psychology of Coaching to the Practice of Leaders

David Webster
CPsychol

 Mc Graw Hill

Open University Press

Open University Press
McGraw Hill
8th Floor, 338 Euston Road
London
England
NW1 3BH

email: enquiries@openup.co.uk
world wide web: www.openup.co.uk

First edition published 2021

A catalogue record of this book is available from the British Library

ISBN-13: 9780335250073
ISBN-10: 0335250076
eISBN: 9780335250080

Library of Congress Cataloging-in-Publication Data
CIP data applied for

Typeset by Transforma Pvt. Ltd., Chennai, India

Praise page

Possibly the best book on teams and coaching I have read. It hits the mark perfectly in terms of being both strongly evidence-based in psychological research, and in covering a hot topic in a readable way.
Jonathan Passmore, Director, Henley Centre for
Coaching & Behavioural Change

Skim-reading this book is almost impossible – there is too much that grabs attention and sucks you in! There are pearls of wisdom on every page which are invaluable to every leader, coach and team. David's generosity in sharing his experience and expertise means there are very practical tools we can all use in our endeavour to learn, improve and innovate in organisations. He makes the complex simple – the true sign of a genius – because he focuses, as always, on the audience or reader and not himself.
Professor Karen Middleton CBE, FCSP, MA, Chief Executive,
The Chartered Society of Physiotherapy

For many years David Webster has been my top recommendation to leaders seeking a world-class team coach, and the depth of his experience and knowledge of team psychology shines through in this thoughtful guide to building team effectiveness in changing times. Whether you're a CEO or CHRO working on team dynamics, or a coach seeking to deepen your practice, you'll find excellent food for thought on every page.
Caroline Webb, Author of global best seller 'How To Have A Good Day' and
Senior Adviser to McKinsey & Company.

David has a profound understanding of what makes teams resilient in change and positioned to perform in the modern world. He also knows how to grant that superpower to others to help them navigate professional and personal change time and again. I know every reader will come to share my gratitude for the lessons these pages hold.
Andrew Shebbeare, Managing Partner, Counteract

A super manual for leaders and teams in all stages of their journey. With context, great insight and practical steps in support and challenge of the team. Leading in a VUCA environment is such a good example. As my coach, and the coach to our coaches at the time, David brings a wonderful intellect, personality and practicality to coaching – and this translates so well into a compelling read.
Niall Myles, SVP Agility, Burrup Hub, Woodside Energy Ltd

For those of us who continually seek to grow our understanding of team and leadership dynamics, and coaching, I wholeheartedly recommend David's book. It's practical and down-to-earth approach, and useful models, interspersed with personal reflections, should especially appeal to those working in the 'front-line' of organisations, who are striving to achieve outstanding performance outcomes, as well as positive, creative and enjoyable team cultures. I certainly appreciated the careful consideration of what might be most valuable and useful in common work-place challenges, evident in the book's structure and concise content. A hugely valuable new resource!

Roland Hamp, Petroleum Engineer and Leadership Coach, Perth, Western Australia

Being lucky to have David as my coach I read this book with great interest and I wasn't disappointed! The book shares all that I have valued in my coaching relationship with David - structure, considered insight, challenge, personal experience, humour and his use of vignettes that are simple and transferable makes this book of value whatever industry you are in. Highly recommended.

Caroline Alexander CBE, Group Chief Nurse, Barts Health NHS Trust

I highly recommend this book. Beautifully written and a joy to read, Creating Adaptive Teams *provides a clear and comprehensive grounding in the essentials of effective team working at the same time as offering original insights and perspectives stemming from the author's considerable experience and expertise. As the world evolves and the challenges and opportunities facing teams become more complex, this insightful and informative text is the companion you will want to reach for - whether you are looking for solutions to problems, seeking new ideas to shape your thinking, or wanting a source of inspiration. I would highly recommend this book to anyone who wants to learn more about creating adaptable teams: whether you are leading them, coaching them, or members of them, it is a resource that you will want to return to, time and time again.*

Professor Sarah Corrie, CPsychol

This is a great book: comprehensive, practical, and well written. Its value comes from the fact that it brings together thorough research and deep experience in one readable volume.

The kind you keep close at hand to dip into when you need help and insight.

Myles Downey, Coach and Author

Contents

List of figures and tables

Figures

Tables

Acknowledgements

This book has truly been a team effort. My wonderful dog walker, Jade, asked me how long it had taken me to write the book. 'About 10 years,' I said. Those of you who sat in on coach development sessions where the demonstration subject was my book will be testament to that. I would like to apologize to all of those people who suffered the interminable call I gave in my desire to write.

I find myself in an Oscar's speech situation. Thanking my mother is a given, and my father, the first to introduce me to organizational theory, and himself a gifted senior leader. I would like to thank Myles Downey from whose shadow I needed to move 20 years ago. My quite extraordinary team at the Centre for Teams, in no particular order: Lauren Hogg, a naturally gifted coach and my closest ally, the human sunshine that is Elana Friedman, Chris Sheepshanks, my very good friend and brilliant business partner for those corpse reviver moments, Gordon Lyle for his ironclad personal and so professional support, Judith Firman for the uncompromising challenges and hilarity, Heidi Ashley for the talent she brings and the jokes we share, Phil Oliver for his brilliance and his friendship, to Tony Page for showing this life was possible, to Charles Brook for his support and friendship and to John Bristow for his confidence-inducing psychological supervision in the early years. Ian and Martin at Red Giant – thank you for understanding the Framework and translating it into a brilliant graphic. Thank you to McGraw-Hill, especially Laura Pacey, Clara Heathcock, and Zoe Osman who have made this book possible. Thank you too to my former wife, Lesley, to whom I apologize for spending most of our marriage on self-improvement, to my son, Edward, a precious and glorious human being, my thanks to them both for their love and support. To my doctor for keeping me alive, and to my wonderful friends for shielding me especially by great friend Rick - thanks for all the geese. And, finally, to my cocker spaniel, Molly, for her unconditional love.

As all coaches know, we learn from and alongside our clients, and I am no exception. I have had the privilege of working with highly talented leaders and great companies – many of whom have demonstrated what a thriving work-place can be like. I would, in particular, like to thank RLG International and Roger Laing, Mike Morgan and Chris Payne who coached and led the brilliant teams I based my research on.

You can all go back home now. Nothing to see here.

Foreword

Dear Lucky Reader,

This book is a gift. It is also an act of great service to teams everywhere. And a well-stocked toolkit waiting for you to pick up and use to make your team better.

Anyone who has worked with David Webster and the Centre for Teams will likely read *Creating Adaptable Teams* as soon as they can. Then re-read it. Then put it on a shelf where they can always reach it for reference. Copies of it will turn up as a gift for friends and colleagues who are desperate to make their team work better, or who are daunted by the idea of leading a new team that has big expectations of them (and itself). Some CEOs – myself included – will bulk order copies for their teams and clients and send them out with notes exhorting them to read it cover to cover.

My team at Brilliant Noise and I have worked with David for seven years now and he has helped us shape how we work with one another, growing our ability to make good decisions, collaborate and, above all, work in service of our team. I credit the lessons he shares in this book with having built the resilience that saw us survive and even improve our company through the novel coronavirus pandemic's great shocks – when so many certainties and resources that we had counted on disappeared in a matter of days.

How teams work with extreme uncertainty is a vital part of our digital consultancy and marketing work for global clients like Barilla, EDF and Universal Studios. So many of the things we have learned with David infused the way that we worked in service of our own clients' success too. Similarly in Brilliant Noise's leaders' work outside of the company, as non-executives and volunteers for charities we have shared the ideas and made use of the toolkit he has given us.

Spending time with David is always a privilege. Whether it is a day-long management retreat or a half-hour Zoom meeting, you always come away with a greater sense of clarity or insight about how you are and how you are working than you started with. The gift of this book, whether you are fortunate enough to meet David and his colleagues at the Centre for Teams or not, is that he has laid out the best of his ideas and experience in a form that will always be there for you, whenever you need it. There is a small stack of books that I keep close to hand when I am working – from here on, this will be one of them.*

The Ten Principles are particularly eye-catching. They are both stimulating and, in the specifics, highly practical. The idea that 'other realities are available'

---

* My current 'Desert Island library' prior to the publication of *Creating Adaptable Teams* comprised *The Hard Thing About Hard Things*, *How to Have a Good Day*, *Dreyer's English*, *The Chambers Dictionary*, *High Output Management*, *Principles*, and *The Economist Style Guide*.

(the wording for which as a team we are proud of having helped shape) has been enormously helpful to us in solving the knotty challenges we have encountered and encouraged us as a team to continue to be open to each other's take, especially on mission critical decisions. It's almost magical when differences are explored and the world shifts before your eyes. It isn't magic, of course; it is a perceptual tool, a way of looking at things that once learned is always there for you.

If you're thinking about reading this book, I hope this foreword encourages you to dive in. It won't change your team in a moment. It will give you every tool you need to change it and grow and achieve more in a world beset by uncertainty and immense challenges. A world that needs teams – and teamship – to meet and overcome those challenges.

Antony Mayfield
CEO of Brilliant Noise, Chair of Lighthouse Arts
Brighton, January 2021

Preface

Acknowledge, adapt and thrive

As I write, we are still to emerge from the depths of a pandemic and have some way to go before the dust settles on massive global change. This unique challenge has caused seismic shifts in the way that teams have operated. Zoom meetings have dominated, along with the psychological requirements of being able to work by yourself without the water cooler conversations to stimulate, the work environment to motivate, and friends and colleagues to play-off and collaborate with. Team leaders have needed to understand how they can attend to the business imperatives while being significantly less in touch with team members. And team members have grappled with staying connected with their colleagues and focusing on the job in hand. This, of course, is compounded if you live in a small flat and have small children who are not going to school.

What has been fascinating is the number of times that 'adapt' has been the watchword – we have all had to adapt to a new way of working individually, teams have had to adapt their response to crisis and recognize when crisis ends and a different 'business as usual' emerges, and organizations have needed to adapt to a critically different financial situation while retaining some semblance of their cultural and operational imperatives. In addition, we have had to adapt to not knowing what the future holds. For many, of course, this has been topped with the need to actually survive financially.

Same challenges, only louder

However, one of our clients captured it well: the challenges and opportunities are the same as they were before, it's just that the volume has been turned up tenfold on them. So, if you had a shaky situation before, you really do now. Crisis and pressure situations tend to show in stark contrast, where one is exposed – and this is true of teams.

Collaboration or competition?

The first few months of 2020 saw evidence of both collaboration as well as competition between local, national and international bodies. Yet for the most part, we are all being reminded of the power of collaboration and collective action to solve complex problems and to stabilize a confusing and challenging environment. We see it all around us and it is inspiring – communities coming together to care for the vulnerable; creativity and innovation in family systems in providing support to each other; a quarter of a million people volunteering to support the NHS; and the Nightingale hospitals being set up to take care of thousands of patients in a few short weeks. Equally, however, we have all seen examples of more competitive, protectionist attitudes dominating, even at a national level, in scrambling to secure medical supplies and equipment. So, we have seen evidence of collective effort writ large both where it is working really well, and where it is not working so well as competition overrides the desire to collaborate.

The pandemic may have shown you what sort of team you are, what your strengths are as a team and where the pinch points lie. Wherever you are on the team-effectiveness spectrum, there are ways of addressing those challenges and ensuring your team does thrive and can sustain its performance over time.

The adaptable team in a virtual/hybrid virtual world

Selectively turn the volume up in response

There are particular elements of the Adaptable Team Framework that are especially important in a virtual or virtual-hybrid team:

- **'Purpose' and 'setting direction':** Because being clear on your new purpose and goal set will lower anxiety and give focus to activity
- **'Psychological safety' and 'trust':** Because together they enable the team to remain healthy and productive
- **'Behavioural expectations':** Because boundaries and clear expectations will support team members to remain focused
- **'Systems and stakeholders', including 'Systems in a VUCA world':** Because the system around every team has changed and will continue to change, and being a student of the system will enable adaptability
- **'Team leadership', especially coaching:** Because great team leadership is central to teams that can adapt and thrive.

Here are 10 observations that will assist teams to thrive in a virtual and hybrid virtual world:

1. **Be super clear on purpose:** Teams that are, can light a 'fire in the belly', and, conversely, teams that fail, do so because they lack a clear purpose (Lipnack and Stamps 1997).
2. **Button down those assumptions:** Not being with colleagues means that it is more important than ever to test assumptions as to agreements, deadlines, goals and next actions.
3. **Distribute leadership:** In a time of uncertainty, leaders need to relinquish control once the course and the rules have been set. This is the time for distributing leadership – it will give the team quicker decision-making and greater responsibility and accountability.

4 **Make it safe:** Continue to make the team a safe place to speak up, disagree, raise the business and the personal challenges. As the leading researcher in the psychological safety field describes it, it is the 'extra ingredient' or kind of 'binding agent'. A series of studies has shown that psychological safety can help overcome geographic dispersion, improve the quality and contribution to decision-making from raising the quality of relationships, and gaining value from increasingly diverse workforces (Edmondson 2019).

5 **Inquire, listen for and acknowledge** mood and emotion. There is talk now of a parallel pandemic, one in which there is psychological collateral damage experienced by large sections of the population whose lives have been turned upside down literally, psychologically or both. Paying attention to how your colleagues are feeling and what they are thinking is good peer and team member support. If you are the leader, acknowledge that everyone will deal with it differently.

6 **Structure:** Give and encourage structure in the working day by agreeing standards of the team, which include behavioural expectations, embracing both work time and downtime during the day. Encourage these structures to ensure there are boundaries, at least in time, if not location, between work and home. Be mindful of the personal space that one enters on a Zoom call.

7 **Coach:** As a leader, focus on your coaching, and in that allow a good separation between 'task' and 'relationship' conversations, the business and the personal check-ins.

8 **Balance communications:** When communicating, ensure that within the team and between the team and those you lead, there is a good balance between good news and less good news. Some friends of mine have stopped listening to the national news so as not to be surrounded by the potential for disaster 24/7.

9 **Give me a break!** In longer meetings and for coaching and workshops, make sure you are breaking the session up to allow collaboration when everybody is together, use breakout rooms to make the conversations more personal and meaningful, keep the session varied with polls, hand raising and perhaps short videos.

10 **Display 'deliberate calm':** The ability to detach from a situation and think clearly about how one will navigate it, the hallmarks of which are humility but not helplessness; and 'bounded optimism' or confidence combined with realism – share your confidence that the team will navigate its way successfully (Brassey and Kruyt 2020).

Who is this book for?

This book is aimed at two principal audience groups. I would like coaches and psychologists who wish to broaden or ground their practice in the field to read this book. In addition, though perhaps first in my mind when I conceived of the book a long time ago, I would like leaders and team members, senior and otherwise, to read this book. I would particularly like leaders and team members to read the book because teams that thrive are central to the health of a modern organization. Somehow, we seem to have lost the art of focusing on our small teams as the real engine-house of a thriving organization. The more that organizations can therefore grasp this opportunity and get really good at it, the better. When, therefore, outside agencies like mine, the Centre for Teams, come in to support the team as team coaches and coaching psychologists, we are working with a prepared (or perhaps usefully curious!) audience. This allows everybody to go further, and to thrive in the quest for high and sustainable results.

How do I read this book?

The book is broadly in three sections:

- Chapters 1–3 look at the Adaptable Team Framework, the fact that all of us have our own experience of team working and group work from our past, and 10 core principles of a truly Adaptable Team, which are useful for both coach and leader as well as team.
- Chapters 4 and 5 look at what you need to do to prepare for your coaching of the team, either as a coach or a leader. We examine the dynamic relationship between coach and team on the key skills that a coach brings to bear on what can be a complex and challenging assignment, but one that brings great rewards.
- Chapters 6–12 bring into focus all of the elements of the Adaptable Team approach and looks at them in detail – focusing on systems and stakeholders, team purpose, the actions of a team, team dynamic, team leadership and team learning rhythm. In that last section, we extend the conversation into the broader field of the learning organization.

If you are a leader who wishes to have an executive summary of the Adaptable Team Framework and its principal contribution, then read the chapter entitled 'The team's journey' (Chapter 1), and then 'Team leadership' (Chapter 11). I would also recommend reading the section on psychological safety within the team dynamic chapter (Chapter 10). If you are a leader who is intending to coach your team, I would recommend reading each chapter, with a focus perhaps on 'Coaching the team' (Chapter 5). If you are a team member in a hurry, I would recommend you read 'The team's journey' – Chapter 1. Each subsequent chapter adds more to your understanding of the Adaptable Team Framework, though specific additional chapters for team members I recommend are 'Team purpose' (Chapter 7), 'Team dynamic' (Chapter 10), and 'Ten core principles of the truly Adaptable Team' (Chapter 3).

If you're a professional coach, I'd invite you to both pick and choose as well as go to chapters that will satisfy your curiosity.

In truth, however, I would wish team members, team leaders and team coaches to read the book cover to cover.

All of our efforts are required to encourage teams to truly thrive.

1 The team's journey

'Happy families are all alike; every unhappy family is unhappy in its own way.'
(*Anna Karenina*, Tolstoy)

Adapt and thrive

If your organization has great teams, you will thrive; your organization will thrive. Teams are the greatest source of competitive advantage for any organization. For many of us, they are the ultimate expression of organizational contribution. They are the reason that we go to work: to perform, to belong, to be appreciated, to find purpose and structure, to learn, to create meaningful change together and to make our particular mark on the world. No one can realize these ambitions alone. It is only when we are leading and working with others effectively and efficiently that we can know our best and most productive selves.

This chapter presents what can be gained by helping teams to adapt and thrive in organizations, and in contrast the cost of teams that just 'get by'. We look at the primary and secondary research that is the basis of a new approach, and the Adaptable Team Framework is then introduced as a blueprint through which teams can be helped to adapt to context and to thrive.

Teams that thrive and those that 'get by'

Great team membership: the ultimate contribution

We have evolved to collaborate, and yet at times don't seem to be very good at it. Our foraging and hunting ancestors learned to collaborate beyond the bounds of family, and we have retained the dominant altruism and collaboration which is the root of our cultural, social and economic lives. We have organized ourselves into teams throughout our history – in peace and war, at home and play, in our family and in our organizations. Teams can be where we find energy and enjoyment through collective endeavour in working towards objectives that we find meaningful. Even in individualistic societies, teams are a catalyst for our ability to express our greatest gifts and ultimate contribution.

It is very difficult to think of anybody, however brilliant, being able to achieve things just by themselves without the support of others or indeed without a team around them. The Sistine Chapel was not painted by Michelangelo alone. Nobel prize-winners collaborate with others. Society, in fact whole civilizations, have been built on working together and this continues to be the case.

We contrast teams that 'thrive' with teams that 'get by'. In today's organization, it is likely that you work with a number of teams, not just one, and the stark reality is that there are some that we take joy in being a part of and contributing to, and others that consistently feel difficult, painful and hard work. Which one are you in?

Teams that thrive

You may recognize the following picture of a team that it's a joy to be part of:

- You meet with colleagues, even virtually, and there is warmth and humour, openness and honesty, and this builds energy, enthusiasm and interest.
- Your peers freely give their support to you and also offer productive challenge and there's enough trust to have difficult conversations.
- Team meetings may be tough, but they provide drive and focus.
- You feel a strong sense of purpose – and there is a meaningful focus on common goals and objectives for which you all hold each other mutually accountable, and that connect to the broader needs the team is serving – those of customers, staff or the wider community.
- You know why you have got up this morning; you know why you are at work today.
- You all take time as a team, to learn together, and to use that learning to adapt to emerging circumstances – and that learning helps you grow and be a better leader.
- You are happy to offer discretionary effort to this team because you feel you belong, and the prize is worth it.
- The team seems to be on an upward spiral – the more you get good results, the quicker you work and the more your results improve.

Vignette: A utility leadership team was able to stabilize a challenging investment delivery schedule while working with a client in significant organizational and cultural change. They established a good foundation of goals and mutual challenge and support and over time developed a high degree of trust between one another, feeling safe enough to address conflict head on and remain on track with performance. Their performance consistently improved over the three years they worked together, becoming easier to sustain even in times of continued change.

Teams that 'get by'

On the flip side, teams can be excruciating environments too:

- You drag yourself to meetings you don't want to be at and question the value of.
- You are low in energy, protective of your time and your good ideas.

- You keep things close to your chest fearing recrimination if you speak up.
- You are exhausted by the lack of focus and prioritization.
- You and your colleagues bury bad news, having the real conversations in the corridor after the meeting.
- You feel it's quicker, safer, to act alone.
- You sense there is destructive conflict not far beneath the surface.

Vignette: The 'leadership committee' of a consultancy firm had been struggling to establish a meaningful purpose for its work together and faced flight risks within and just beyond the team. Workloads were felt to be onerous and well-being difficult to maintain. Team members were keeping individual focus by having bi-laterals away from the team meetings, but as a result struggled to overcome a feeling of disconnection between departments, giving rise to ongoing challenges in delivering business as usual and change when required.

Paragraph While it is our experience that it is easy to say 'this is just how it is', and at some level become resigned to the nature of the team that we are a part of, our experience is that it really doesn't have to be that way – and for your own sake, and the sake of the team and the organization, it does not have to be left to chance. Most teams, whether they are short-lived or long term, carry big responsibilities. Team effectiveness, and the fact that teams are a joy to be a part of, can never be guaranteed unless you mindfully work at it.

This means senior leaders need to know how to lead small teams, and team members need to be aware of how they can most effectively and quickly contribute; it is incumbent upon both the leadership and the team members to root out opportunities to improve the collective effort so that teams can in reality become the ultimate expression of organizational contribution – and not a waste of time and an utterly dismal experience full of opportunities for ill-health.

Organizations need to take a stand on teams on their watch, and actively address how they can become more effective, adaptable and high performing. As my father was fond of saying, 'nothing is inevitable except death and taxes'. So it is with teams – these benefits are not guaranteed. In fact, an extensive study of a variety of teams (Hackman 1990) led the researchers to conclude that high performance teams are not the norm, they are the exception.

What are the benefits of thriving teams in organizations?

The benefits of effective teams are now well rehearsed but worth repeating here, as we seek to keep our 'eyes on the prize', as one of my clients would say.

- **Raise productivity:** From coal mine to sales team, good teams raise productivity (Trist et al. 1977; Macy and Izumi 1993; Wisner and Feist 2001).
- **Build quality:** In manufacturing, teams have been shown to 'build quality' into the process (Glassop 2002).

- **Reduction in errors:** 43–70% of malpractice in the US has resulted from poor teamwork (Lewis and Tully 2009).
- **Improved patient safety** from effective team dynamics, which encourages team members to raise important issues (Nembhard and Edmondson 2006).
- **Increased innovation** (Fay et al. 2006).

Importantly for today's environment, there are also huge psychological and socio-emotional benefits:

- Team members gain a sense of belonging (Baumeister and Leary 1995).
- Team members experience more positive attitudes than those working alone, a greater sense of well-being, and reduced uncertainty (Pearson 1992; Wall et al. 1986).
- Where teams across the organization work well together, the performance of the organization is more than the sum of individual teams.

What is the cost of poor teamship?

In our business we use the collective term 'teamship' to encapsulate what enables the organization to thrive and to achieve successful results through effective collective endeavour. In a team, it means having a compelling common purpose that aligns with stakeholder need, nurturing a healthy and effective team dynamic, ensuring first-class and co-ordinated action, and ensuring continuous team learning. For an organization, it means the alignment and effective collaboration across boundaries to create, in effect, a learning organization. For team leaders and team members, it requires the skills, capabilities, mindset and behaviours that enable all of this to happen.

The upside of teamship when applied appropriately is that individuals and organizations thrive. There is a huge opportunity cost in not ensuring that teams thrive both at an individual and a whole enterprise level. It is useful also to consider the impact of poor teamship on well-being. Recent Gallup research (2019) has identified what they describe as 'the well-being five' – five areas of one's life that are useful to focus on in creating well-being – career, social, financial, community and physical. Because of the amount of time spent at work, they are all impacted by one's experience in one's job. They describe career as liking what you do each day and being motivated to achieve goals. They go on to say that there is a '48% greater likelihood that people with low engagement and wellbeing will leave your company'. In addition, there are '7/10 millennials who experience at least some burnout on the job'. Finally, there is a '15% greater likelihood that direct reports will be thriving in wellbeing when their manager is thriving in well-being' – so an important lesson there for team leaders. It is also interesting to note that the most recent research on this topic (Gandhi & Robison (2020)) tells us that 'since the pandemic started no more than 52% have strongly agreed that their organization cares about their overall well-being – this was down to 46% in mid-July'. Research on engagement also puts the cost of a disengaged employee at between $3,400 and $10,000 – and this would be substantially more for the senior-most leaders – and it is no guarantee that a senior leader's innate conscientiousness would see them through – they are more likely to be a flight risk.

What gets in the way of teams learning to thrive?

We ask this of teams as part of the coaching process, and these are some of things that they tell us:

- We don't know where to start.
- The team moves so fast – we have no time to slow down and address this stuff.
- We focus solely on the task or end results, without being mindful of the need to develop a strong process that enables us to achieve it together.
- We know it's team dynamics but that's a bit daunting to address.
- We feel vulnerable or even fearful of speaking up and addressing difficult issues within the team that are impacting its ability to perform well; instead, we opt for an easier life (that is, in fact, not so easy).
- There is a power dynamic – where it's hard to challenge the leader.
- There is an elephant in the room – and we can't talk about it for fear of everything unravelling.
- Our real conversations take place in the corridor after the meeting – not in it – so there is no collective understanding.
- People here are tired and worn down – and so accept a sub-optimal situation.
- Our organizational culture does not welcome collaboration.
- We don't feel we have permission from above or indeed around us to address these issues – and that it may be interpreted as a sign of weakness that we cannot just sort them out ourselves.

Our experience is that all of these challenges can be addressed, but only if leaders and team members have the courage to do so. Our observation is that many teams muddle along. Teamship is simply left to chance, or to the hope that if we stick eight talented individuals together in a room, they will immediately work well together. This can be okay until a real challenge or crisis emerges, by which time our experience is that things often unravel. However, as my favourite book title by a US Army General has it, *Hope Is Not a Strategy*. And at times, it is very useful to have some help in the form of professional coaching for the team to gain the benefits, even if they are senior (or perhaps especially if they are senior teams given the impact senior teams have), as 'high spirited, independent minded thoroughbreds are often convinced of the rightness of their ways and are not responsive to correction – even by the lead horse' (Wageman et al. 2008, xvii).

Vignette: One organization in the creative sector was full of anxiety. Team members were working long hours and exhausted by the whole thing. The new chief executive bought us in to analyse the situation and make recommendations. Our recommendation was brief: a simple set of goals, limited in number and easy to measure, along with a regular heartbeat of meetings around those goals – this made a huge difference to their ability to function. And they found themselves learning quickly how to lead the organization spread over three continents, full of ambitious, bright young people.

Roots of the Adaptable Team Framework

Teams and the effectiveness journey

We conducted research in 2008 that sought to take a fresh look at a team's journey towards effectiveness and help leaders, practitioners and team members alike to be clear on the critical factors that will lead to great output, personal growth and development of the team's capacity to deliver in the future.

Some definitions to help us

- **What is a team?** The definition of a team to be used here is taken from Hackman (1987, 315–342): 'a team is a collection of individuals who are interdependent in their tasks, who share responsibility for outcomes, who see themselves and who are seen by others as an intact social identity embedded in one or more larger social systems, and who manage their relationships across organisational boundaries'.
- **Two principal team types:** A leadership team 'shares responsibility for the success of (a part of) the firm' (Cohen and Bailey 1997, 241). Project teams are 'time-limited' teams, producing one-time outputs and involving 'considerable application of knowledge, judgement and expertise' (Cohen and Bailey 1997, 241).
- **What is team effectiveness?** Team 'effectiveness' is defined by Hackman (1990) as: the productive output of the team (as assessed by clients of the team); the enhanced capability of the team to perform interdependently in the future; the individual learning, growth and personal well-being of individual team members.

The current models

It is useful to point out that the Adaptable Team Framework seeks to build on the models that came before it and is a product of both desk and field research as well as practice and experience. Each of the models below is valuable in its own right; they all teach us something about teams and are very helpful for the professional coach to explore. So, the different models seeking to convey the journey of a team towards effectiveness are as follows:

Figure 1.1 The Staged Approach
(Created by author from text: Tuckman 1965)

Group Structure	Testing and dependence	Intra-group conflict	Development of group cohesion	Functional-role relatedness	Separation
	Forming	**Storming**	**Norming**	**Performing**	**Adjourning**
Task	Orientation to the task	Emotional response to the task	Open exchange of relevant interpretations	Emergence of solutions	Review Ending

The staged approach to group development, developed by Bruce Tuckman in 1965, is best known by its descriptive headings 'forming, storming, norming, performing and adjourning' (Figure 1.1). He classified the stages of development by 'task' (goal) and 'group structure' (relationships), drawing on problem-solving theory and psychodynamics. Despite it dominating the last 40 years of team development work, it is flawed: it makes no mention of the context in which the group operates; it does not tell us anything about the duration of the stages or of the triggers that shift the team from one stage to another; it assumes inevitable improvement and is founded mainly on therapy groups.

Punctuated equilibrium, developed by Connie Gersick in 1988, is founded on laboratory and real-world research and proposes that groups progress through two phases. She observed that the first phase was started by the first meeting, which established a working pattern and a plan of activities. Halfway (in time) through the life of the group, phase one work and approaches were abandoned; a sense of urgency emerged, as the groups focused on the deadline and began to engage meaningfully with the others outside the group and with information obtained from outside the group. This drove a fresh way of working, a new approach and a new direction, which they then maintained throughout phase two until completion – the time at which the group's output was prepared for external consumption. Gersick's work has three distinct benefits: It was a study of 'naturally occurring work teams' so has the potential to be more useful to organizations (Hackman and Wageman 2005). The real-world setting allowed context to appear as a variable. It takes account of time as a variable.

Marks, Mathieu and Zaccaro (2001, 358) propose that team development is a series of **'input, process, output (I-P-O) episodes,'** where 'time-based rhythms act to shape how teams manage their behavior' between two phases: 'action' ('acts that contribute directly to goal accomplishment') and 'transition' (planning and evaluation). The result is a series of action and transition movements starting and finishing at different times, running in parallel. The idea of 'time-based rhythm' is an attractive one. It recurs throughout the work of a leading teams academic, Richard Hackman (1990), and his study of seven different

Figure 1.2 Punctuated Equilibrium
(Created by author from text: Gersick 1988)

Equilibrium 1	Equilibrium 2
Strategy one selected	Strategy two selected
Agreement and disagreement	Urgency
Certainty and uncertainty	Change of plan / direction
Leader / team in step and out of step	Re-ordering with context
Acceptance or rejection of project	Much detail
	Decline if conflict not addressed

types of teams. Perhaps this is most clearly signalled in relation to performing groups (theatre and athletic groups) where the 'rhythmic variation is expressed concretely in the performance, in the pacing and intensity of the game, in the dialogue, in musical phrasings . . . intensity builds until released in the catharsis of performance' (1990, 281).

A modern developmental sequence. In the 1980s and 1990s, Katzenbach and Smith's (1993) 'Wisdom of Teams' proposed that teams could be categorized according to where they are on a developmental spectrum. The spectrum moves from working group, pseudo-team, potential team and real team to high-performing team. Within each, there could be said to be the same distinction that Tuckman made between the two realms of task and structure. Their qualitative study of 50 teams is persuasive.

The Adaptable Team: field study

This study posed the question, 'what does a team need to do over time to be effective?' Two 'effective' teams in the oil and gas industry were studied, using a grounded theory approach (one that aimed to build theory, starting with no preconceived notion of the data that would emerge). Data collection was carried out using the Critical Incident Technique in 15 one-to-one interviews in April 2008. Both were highly successful teams – one an Asset Leadership team in the North Sea oil and gas sector; the other a Project Team working in Russia, which saved their client over $250 million in their two-year project. Both were led or coached by RLG International, based in Vancouver. Iterative reviews of the 19 hours of transcription yielded two case studies and then key themes or activities in which the teams engaged. The themes were compared to existing staged models, which are described above, and a new model emerged based on the High Performance Cycle (within Goal Setting Theory) from which the Adaptable Team Model was created.

What we found

We found that the teams carried out the following in their quest for effectiveness. They:

1 Set **core team goals.** They comprised long-term aspirations, short-term output goals, process goals and, for some, learning goals.

2 Ensured **feedback** on performance and behaviour from within and outside the team was obtained and used to adjust activity towards the goals. For one team this triggered 'relentless follow-up'.

3 Developed confidence and belief (**potency**). This played a huge part in the effectiveness of the teams. Its absence had a deleterious effect on team performance.

4 Continually reviewed and created **strategies** for goal attainment.

5 Developed actual or perceived **interdependence** – a reliance on other team members to complete tasks, to learn, to grow.

6 Built sufficient **mutual trust**. Each of the teams invested time in building relationships. As a result of greater trust, each team could build their own unique understanding of mutual accountability, though some were more successful at maintaining it than others.

7 Benefited from **the leader**. All the leaders displayed belief in the possibility of team success from the off, as well as in their ability to lead.

8 Carried out **team learning** – real-time learning as a result of real issues was a key theme in all teams and appeared to contribute directly to effectiveness. One team leader commented that 'day-to-day coaching and spending time with Shackleton [a text they used] works far better than any of this nonsense about going on a training course.'

Patterns of the team studied

The teams studied exhibited a pattern of an incremental **virtuous cycle** of team goal setting, strategizing, progress and then confidence. Both the teams set **team goals** – 'proximal' and 'distal' – and they set explicit and implicit **learning goals**, respectively. These offered team members a **choice** and **direction**. The goals galvanized team **effort** and **persistence** and drove continual **strategizing**. **Emergent performance** gave team members opportunities to **re-commit**. Continual **feedback** on performance and behaviour was critical in the teams' **ability to self-regulate**; **self-efficacy** (confidence) at an individual level and **potency** (belief) at a team level were strengthened as a direct result of having overcome substantial challenges. Where these elements were lacking, team effectiveness appeared to suffer.

How this compared to the previous models above

- Current models could not fully explain the journey of the teams that we had looked at.
- The 'staged model' (Tuckman) was in evidence, but the stages did not occur in order and effectiveness was by no means inevitable. Context (absent from the staged model) played a crucial part in all the teams' journeys.
- Punctuated equilibrium was not observed in full.
- All teams did, however, generate a 'rhythm' of activity and where it was less evident, the team became less effective.

We therefore created a new 'lens', which over time became the Adaptable Team Framework.

Locke and Latham's (2002) High Performance Cycle, contained within their Goal Setting Theory (GST), was felt to provide the best fit with the data gathered. The Cycle and GST are focused mainly on individual motivation and remain surprisingly less tested in a team environment. GST, however, is 'among the most valid and practical theories of employee motivation in organizational psychology' (Locke and Latham 2002, 714).

For managers and practitioners, the Adaptable Team cycle offers a simple set of recommendations and a map for team effectiveness: set team goals – long term and short term performance and learning goals, ensure the mechanisms are in place to plan and execute, and incrementally check in with and build on the moderators of performance and learning – especially 'potency'. This may require an exploration of what is happening subconsciously that may be slowing progress. Also, track effectiveness on output, team capability and individual learning. Periodically stop and ensure a willingness to commit to the next stage. Ensure that you (the leader) are learning and encouraging the team to learn 'live' and solve problems together. The practitioner's ability to aid a team to learn live appeared to be particularly crucial.

Adaptable Team Framework

How to adapt and thrive: the Adaptable Team Framework

When leading, participating in and coaching a team, it is useful to have a routemap, a way of helping each other navigate each of the areas that will ultimately contribute to a team that thrives and creates sustainable performance over time. This is what we set out to do as part of our research and the creation of the Adaptable Team Framework. We have adjusted the approach through our experience over the last 12 years and consolidated a quantitative and qualitative assessment to aid teams and their coaches. The genesis of the model and the threads that reach back into the desk research follows the explanation of the framework itself.

The model comprises eight key elements, each of which we shall unpack in the rest of the book sharing pointers and orientation as well as the research that will help teams and coaches engage effectively in productive conversation that will contribute to team success. Those eight key elements are as follows:

1 Stakeholders
2 Purpose
3 Results
4 Actions
5 Dynamic
6 Team learning rhythm
7 Team leadership
8 Learning organization

Clearly, the last element is about the organization as a whole but our proposition, as you would imagine, is that the more you connect teams that thrive across an organization the more you create the opportunity for the whole organization to thrive, and learning is a critical element in being able to adapt, improve and create sustainable results.

Here's a pen sketch of each of these elements. Subsequent chapters will take each element and expand it in more detail.

Stakeholders

At the heart of the activity of any team is what stakeholders require of that team. These stakeholders come in a variety of different forms and in effect constitute the system within which the team operates. Examples of internal stakeholders could be staff, other teams, the board, the executive team and

Figure 1.3 The Adaptable Team: Core Components
Graphic by Red Giant, London

specialist functions. Examples of external stakeholders include customers, their communities, local and national government, and regulators. These internal and external stakeholders, to a greater or lesser extent, require something of the team. And this is the team's primary task – to understand what those stakeholders do require. This is the system – a complex web of groups and agencies that have a constantly shifting dynamic between them. We will discuss the idea of stakeholders as participating in a system in a later chapter.

Purpose

The clarity and sense of purpose and identity that the team has around its work together is a central tenet for the Adaptable Team. This might not be the starting place for some teams, but it certainly is a crucial element in team success. The purpose is a direct function of stakeholder expectations. It is also a function of what the team thinks and feels is important to deliver on in service of stakeholder expectations. It is therefore crucial that the purpose of the team, and its stakeholders are all aligned.

Once the team's purpose is clear, it is much easier to be clear on the results the team wishes to create – to set meaningful goals that will focus its attention on outputs and outcomes.

Results

The results the team gets are more than just what is often described as its performance – its metrics. When we talk about results, we talk about four different kinds of outcomes and outputs that the team can usefully measure its progress by. The first of these of course is performance – the output that is required and the kinds of outcomes that accrue from those outputs. Examples include revenue targets, deadlines, health and safety targets, and the like. In addition to performance, we would invite the team to examine three other areas.

The first is learning – is the team continuing to learn from its own experience of seeking to deliver in context? If learning or the quality of learning declines, the team might be said to be failing to innovate and adapt effectively or as swiftly as it needs to. It's important therefore that the team observes the degree of learning it is experiencing.

The next is enjoyment – is the team enjoying its work together such that team members actually want to continue to contribute? Clearly, if every day for team members is like a pride-swallowing siege and nobody enjoys being part of the team, then performance will eventually decline – however good it might be in one moment.

Finally, contribution – is the work of the team generating a sense of meaningful endeavour for team members such that they want to continue to contribute? By meaningful endeavour we mean the desire to contribute beyond your own needs and wants, over time.

Actions

Being clear on the purpose of the team and results that you want is, of course, only the initial step. The team has to actually do things, engage in action in order to be able to produce those results, and that action has to be coordinated and thought through in order to be effective and efficient. The team needs to be really good at setting direction and goals that can guide the team's activity, agreeing roles that are clear and delineated, making sound decisions along the way, innovating where necessary and spotting the opportunities for new thinking, creating mutual accountability, making good sense of the differences in experiences and skills that can make the team more successful, and supporting and challenging each other to get the best from each team member.

Dynamic

The quality of those actions that the team engages in in order to produce the results has its roots in the team dynamic. Team dynamic is often something that a team might talk about, but not necessarily know how to address. By team dynamic we mean the hidden forces, both helpful and less helpful, that go to make up how a team thinks and feels and indeed how team members think and feel about each other, the team, and its tasks. Team dynamic is about being a team, sharing emotions and thoughts experienced in relation to the task. This will help the team stay connected, aligned and pulling in the same direction. This is about those things that lie beneath the surface that require sufficient alignment for the coordinated action to be possible. It requires the team to examine if it has:

- **Alignment on behaviours and values:** That is to say expectations of how team members will behave towards each other and what they collectively see as important.
- **Commitment and belief:** Whether team members feel that they will be successful and whether they are committed to the team's endeavours has a material and a statistical influence on success.
- **Sufficient trust:** Such that team members feel that they can rely on each other.
- **A safe environment**, where team members can speak up and solve problems together, without fear of ridicule or recrimination. This last one is perhaps the most important.

Team learning rhythm

In the way that we have been describing stakeholder expectations, results, actions, dynamic and purpose, you will see that there is an intimate relationship between each of these elements that go to make up the team's work. There is also an interplay and dynamic between them. Over time, therefore, we see it is crucial that the team engages in what we would describe as a 'team learning rhythm'. Organizations are very familiar with the idea of an operational rhythm – for example, a rhythm that punctuates the financial period into months, quarters and year end. And often the team will structure meetings in order to be synchronized with those reporting processes. Those operational conversations are an opportunity to look back and to look forwards and focus primarily on the actions that the team takes on the results that it wants. We also encourage a team to engage in a team learning rhythm alongside its operational rhythm in order that it can continue to learn from its own experience and go a bit deeper in those conversations. With a refreshed view of the effect that clarity of purpose and alignment with stakeholders has and awareness of the dynamic of the team being so crucial, we know that team members gain a huge opportunity to learn individually and collectively about how the team can more effectively and efficiently deliver sustainable results. This is really about learning from the team's own experience and developing within the team the capacity to reflect both internally and externally, on relationships as well as the task. The team can learn the kind of actions it needs to take in order to be able to deliver results. But it can also go deeper and understand how the dynamic might be affecting the quality of those actions and indeed how the clarity of purpose and alignment with stakeholders can affect its dynamic and therefore ultimately again the sustainability of results.

Team leadership

Holding all of this together is team leadership. There is clearly an important dynamic between the team leader and team members. There are also three elements of the team leader's role that need to be present for the team leader to get most out of the team and team members to get the most out of themselves and each other. We would describe the three things as leadership, management and coaching. By leadership we mean setting the longer-term direction and engaging the team in that direction. Leadership is really about putting a fire in the belly of team members by engagement with a clear purpose. By management we mean ensuring compliance with agreed standards, rules, agreements and expectations, and objectives and measures put in place to track the team's progress. Management is really about compliance. The third element of the team leader's role we see as being coaching. You may expect that from a coaching book, but it is clear to see that the team leader who believes that they have all the answers without reference to the team, is likely to fail given the complexity of modern organizational life and the need to constantly adapt. Coaching is about supporting and challenging the team to learn and perform to its best.

Learning organization

Up to this point, we have been describing the life of the team in relation to its stakeholders and ensuring good alignment within the team and between the team and its stakeholder groups. If there are a number of teams engaging in this kind of work in order to be able to create high and sustainable performance over time, then the destination becomes an organization that is continuously learning how to improve its performance and ensure that it is sustainable. We use the term learning organization to describe team-to-team performance – a network of teams that go to make up the organization and its ability to learn and perform together.

So, these are the key elements that a coach and a team can, together, focus attention on. We shall look at the roots of these elements in subsequent chapters.

As a result of each part of the Framework, we have devised seven questions for Adaptable Teams to use in any team that is seeking to thrive (and we have developed a more detailed quantitative and qualitative Adaptable Team Assessment at the Centre for Teams from which these questions are derived):

1 **Stakeholders:** What do our internal and external stakeholders want from me and this team?
2 **Purpose:** What, therefore, is our purpose within the system that we serve?
3 **Results:** What do we need to achieve together as a team?
4 **Action:** What do we need to do well together to create those results?
5 **Dynamic:** What do we expect of each other and what kind of dynamic do we need and want?
6 **Rhythm:** What operational and learning rhythm best supports us?
7 **Leadership:** What is my role and where can I make the greatest contribution?

Summary

- Teams that thrive are the building blocks of organizational success. They are more productive, produce work of greater quality and, importantly, can adapt more swiftly to changing contexts.
- Teams that get by struggle to establish a virtuous cycle of performance, lacking direction, focus and a healthy dynamic.
- The Adaptable Team Framework, born out of primary and secondary research, is a systemic approach that helps teams navigate their way towards adapting and thriving in complex modern organizations ensuring sustainable results and healthier team members.
- It focuses attention on critical elements of teamship: stakeholders, purpose, results, action, dynamic, rhythm, leadership.

2 A team member's journey

Devotions upon emergent occasions
No man is an island, entire of itself; every man
is a piece of the continent, a part of the main;
if a clod be washed away by the sea, Europe
is the less, as well as if a promontory were, as
well as if a manor of thy friend's or of thine
own were; any man's death diminishes me,
because I am involved in mankind.
And therefore never send to know for whom
the bell tolls; it tolls for thee.

John Donne, 1624
Metaphysical poet, priest

We all bring ourselves

When we join a team, we don't just bring our technical expertise and experience. We bring all of the threads of our personal history with us into the room – all of those things that make us who we are to that point. We often talk about 'knowing where people are coming from'. This figure of speech is full of richness. Knowing 'where you are coming from' – understanding what has made you who you are and how that can help and hinder a team – is a personal responsibility.

This chapter contains elements of my personal story from family member to occupational and coaching psychologist in order to shed light on the personal nature of our relationship with teams. The aim is to help you reflect on your own team-related story and enable your fullest contribution to teams whether as coach, leader or team member.

A personal story

Our personality and our experiences shape our relationships with groups and teams.
This is a more personal chapter than one might expect in a work-related book because when we come into a team as team leader or team member – or even as coach – we bring all of our life experiences with us. The influence of our past and of our hidden psyche is part of modern discourse, mainly thanks to Freud and Jung. The interaction of those personal drivers from

our subconscious, that can be deeply rooted in our past, can pop up at any time in the present. They may serve to distort our response to those we are with. Being aware of that hidden (psycho-)dynamic within us all is very helpful. Kets de Fries (2012), professor of leadership development and organizational change at INSEAD and a current champion of the psychodynamic approach in organizations, talks about 'a rich tragedy-comedy playing out on our inner stage' where 'to make sense of our behaviour, we must explore our interpersonal history' with significant players in our upbringing. Using those experiences to be effective will help you and help others. A team can be a highly pressurized environment and very rewarding too. That pressure can drive out thoughts and feelings of which, to that point, we had been much less aware. Being a team coach, leading a team and being a team member, I would argue, requires us to be highly self-aware, sensitive to our relationship with teams so we can make our greatest contribution and experience the teams we support and are in, as fulfilling. So, this chapter is to share my own reflections of my journey with teams and towards supporting them as an occupational and coaching psychologist. Whether you are a team leader or a team coach, I would invite you to do the same.

A personal relationship with teams

I am very selective in the groups that I join, the teams that I am part of. This is a combination of my personality and my life experience. I believe we are all circumspect in one way or another.

Families are the first experience we all have of doing things with others and being with others over an extended period of time, and the old adage you can't choose your relatives can occasionally come to mind. It always amazes me how much of an imprint in role and relationship was made at an early age with my family. Although when together, each of us can sustain our adult selves for a couple of days, more than that and there is noticeable regression! The assumptions, cues and habits revisit us, sometimes in a beautifully helpful and joyful way, and sometimes less so. This, of course, should not surprise us. Freud first introduced us to the ideas of psychodynamics and the influence of childhood on our adult selves over a century ago. My work on collaboration, conflict, organization and my relationship with authority, have all been influenced by my early upbringing – refined since but certainly influenced by my past.

School had also taught me a lot about teams, and how teams become more successful, as well as a lot about being an independent individual in a group – which is as I found out later, an early stage in group development (Bennis 1951). When at school, there was a seminal moment that set the course towards teamship for me for the rest of my life. I was the editor of the house magazine and had written an editorial piece that, though a bit precocious, did display how I felt – that if we could all work together more effectively and reduce the angst and conflict between different groups in the school (and by implication in society), life would be better. The subject matter I was citing was the recent house rugby tournament (amusingly called 'Cock House Cup', for a reason that escapes me now), which my house had valiantly lost that year. Miraculously, we had cobbled together a team that was a combination of people with two left feet and some of us who knew how to play. We had lost by the smallest margin. A 'pyrrhic' victory maybe, but a significant step for us and, as it turned out, for me. Returning to the house after our narrow defeat, covered in mud but happy that we had all to a person played out of our skins, I remember the feeling of satisfied exhaustion. We had done something special together. Something more than displaying our rugby talent – there was team spirit, a connection between team members, a respect for talent as well as effort – it was not to do with our representing the house, it was a bond between us as young adults. So, I wrote the article, and reflected on that experience and its implications. I was shocked by the reaction from some: it was swiftly denounced by some teachers as 'jingoistic nonsense'. I know now that there is always a tension between the individual and collective view; it is a delicate balance and the fear of getting lost in the crowd is, for some, overwhelming.

Looking back at my school days, much of the measured response I have to teams stems from that time. Years later, I would find Will Schutz's Human Element's personality theories and, in particular, the FIRO approach, helpful. Developed in the early 1950s through his work with teams in the US Navy engaged in the Korean War, it is now one of the most widely used preference profiles globally and is deployed to both aid individual leaders and team effectiveness. In 'FIRO B' – Fundamental Interpersonal Relations Orientation and 'B' for Behaviour – he identifies three areas of interpersonal need:

- The need for inclusion, indicating how much you generally include other people in your life and how much attention, contact and recognition you want from others. Words associated with inclusion are participation, belonging and togetherness.
- The need for control indicates how much influence and responsibility you want and how much you want others to lead and influence you. Words associated with control include leadership, influence and power.
- The need for affection indicates how close and warm you are with others and how close and warm you want others to be with you – that is to say, what depth of relationship do you wish. Words associated with this need include care, rapport and closeness.

It is useful to reflect on your preferred balance in each of these areas of interpersonal need – how much do you include and want to be included by others in the team? How much control do you want to exert on others and how much you wish others to exert over you? How much affection or what depth of relationship do you wish to have with others and others with you? Reflecting on these both as team member and team leader as well as coach is very helpful in developing your ability to engage with others effectively. Not only does it support you in getting the right balance for yourself, but it makes you a more effective coach by expanding your ability to engage with an expanded repertoire of 'relating', as the team requires. My own need for inclusion is relatively low; the highest need I have is for affection. I have been both accepting of this pattern and challenging myself along with many other elements of data and feedback over the years in order to continue to grow my capability, as a professional and a human being.

Important people, important relationships

For as long as I can remember, I had wanted to join the army. My uncle who I admired for his leadership presence and sense of humour, and to whom I was very close, was, by the mid-1970s, a brigadier. He had seen action in Korea and would go on to head up logistics around the time of the Falklands War as a General. Whatever one might have thought about the politics, the army life appealed. I was hugely attracted to the physical outdoor life, to being in challenging circumstances, and, most of all, to gaining a huge amount of leadership experience at a very early age. From an early age, precociousness encouraged me to organize my willing friends into a regiment and we would go on military expeditions, creating dugouts in the garden and ambushes of unsuspecting adults. Despite this, I decided against joining the military, a decision I often reflect upon. At the time, I would say that I wanted more autonomy and independence. I suspect that I was just not sufficiently confident.

I joined Price Waterhouse in 1988 after university, and though it was a lucky escape for all concerned that I left before I qualified – I would have been a terrible accountant – I thoroughly enjoyed my time there. I was in an 'audit team one', which was itself broken up into three or four small groups assigned to different clients. Each of the smaller teams had a senior, and mine was Richard, a bright, handsome, articulate and fun 'compadre'. He took me under his wing, and we did a number of audits together interspersed with visits to the pub and trips out in his Alfa Spider, which he drove significantly too fast around the London streets. Richard and I and the other team members went into firms, and met with the partner from Price Waterhouse and the client finance director to size up the audit. As a team we created scope and focus and a series of principal activities, and we were off. Given that I knew absolutely nothing about accounting and not much in the way of how an audit was performed, I learned as I went. And yes, the old adage of counting Brillo Pads as a junior auditor is on the money. I counted bricks, I counted pallets of paper, I counted money flows from one account to another and financial positions, and throughout the team was supportive, instructive and we had a lot of fun – and a lot of beer was drunk. At the end of this team effort, which would often take between three weeks and three months, we would file a report and sign off the accounts if appropriate. Occasionally, I was invited into the meeting with the finance director at the end of the audit. For me, this was the most exciting part – it was where the human elements of collective effort met the scoreboard. I was fascinated to see which teams did well in the client's businesses and which teams did not, and frequently the finance director would be curious about exactly the same thing, poised to report to his colleagues not just that trading had been accurately reflected in the accounts but what contributed to the trading position.

Fast forward over the rather difficult conversation I had with my father on leaving Price Waterhouse and you would have found me within Trust House Forte where I worked for three years, helping manage restaurants and catering units as diverse as Newport Pagnell service area, pizzeria franchises and fashionable Soho restaurants. This was a baptism of fire both for my leadership of others as well as for my teamship. As a general manager in retail, you would know how a team was performing hour by hour, as they kept up with service or didn't. The look on their faces, even the take on each shift, varied depending on the quality of the team you had. And the customers would tell you whether they were having a good experience both by the way that they were as well as directly in the tip. All of this is to do with staff teamship.

In 2008 I qualified as an occupational psychologist – late in the game at 42 but it completed a journey that I think had been rumbling on since I was around 16. I had been fascinated by the way that people behaved especially when they were together, their challenges, their thought processes, their motivations and what they felt important. I had joined Myles Downey and his newly formed consultancy business in 1997, one I went on to lead and that was one of the first coach development businesses in Europe at that time and the first to offer accreditation. However, when I had been coaching, I had always been drawn to understand more about the theories that I knew much less about than I felt I should or indeed would like to know. So, I went back to the body of knowledge from which we all, as coaches, draw. In my studies I sought out everything I could find on teams, and in the intervening period, I honed and gathered and learnt with my colleagues and with clients. This book is the product of a journey that has lasted a good 20 years, years in which the coaching of teams has been an endless source of personal and professional fascination and of huge satisfaction.

Reflection questions to assist you

It is useful to reflect on our past when we work in and with teams. Those important relationships from our past such as those I have described above, and unfinished experiences and emotions remain to influence our future selves even if we are unaware of them. They can do this most commonly in two principal ways, transference and projection. Transference is subconsciously transferring the qualities of one relationship to another. Confusing your boss with a father figure for instance, or overbearing colleague with an older sister. Projection (from Freud and then Melanie Klein) is where one takes an aspect of oneself with which one is less comfortable and projects it onto another. For example, saying a colleague is disorganized when it is you who are so. Watching for these moments of psychological confusion is very helpful. Even if you do not declare it to others, being aware of when you are driven by the past and making unhelpful 'assumptions' about others is instructive and can serve to improve working relationships with team members; and if you are a coach, they serve to keep your line of sight clear.

- How much did family members or early groups you were part of share what they thought, what they felt, what they wanted from each other?
- In your early life with whom do you identify most and why?
- How did your family or early groups that you were part of respond to conflict and risk?
- What roles did you play in your family or other group settings, and how does that compare to the role you play in teams at work now?
- Which teams have you enjoyed most and why?
- When you first come into a team what's your initial reaction to being there? How does that change over time?

This volume is the product of continuous exploration and my work with teams before and since the mid 1990s when I started my professional life as a coach to teams. It is aimed at senior team leaders, senior team members and those who coach teams professionally. I hope to provide support to all parties. I know when the team coaching I am engaged in, is doing its job – it's when everyone in the room is in the same conversation, with everyone leaning in with energy and curiosity, hungry to learn and make a difference. I hope this book serves as a resource to help that happen more frequently for all.

Summary

- In working with teams, it is important to be aware of our own interior world and the significant experiences and relationships that have formed us and continue to influence our behaviour towards others.
- This psychodynamic approach to working in organizations allows us to continue to learn and be evermore capable in and around teams.
- We shared some useful questions to help you start to reflect on your own relationship with teams.

3 Ten core principles of the truly Adaptable Team

Universal principles for teamship

It is incumbent upon all of us who work in teams and alongside them to be acutely aware of the filters through which one sees the world and how that affects the contribution that we can make. The 10 core principles of the truly Adaptable Team are for all of us who work in and alongside teams. They are carefully crafted lenses that can help teams be significantly more effective. Without them it will be difficult to function effectively as a coach or leader in a modern complex organization.

The 10 core principles are each described, along with how they show up in practice in tools and in useful questions.

The core principles

The 10 core principles of the truly Adaptable Team

The 10 core principles of the truly Adaptable Team will help you and the teams that you work in and alongside to be more effective. Those core principles are:

1 All things are connected.
2 Slow down to speed up.
3 It's loops, not lines.
4 Be aware of rackets.
5 Be on purpose.
6 Other realities are available.
7 Locate and nurture what's working.
8 We are all systems leaders.
9 Enrol others for lasting change.
10 Remember rule No. 6.

Here are the 10 core principles of working in and supporting a team, as leader and coach as well as team members. They have been developed as a result of years of practice with teams, along with the psychological theory and evidence base to be discussed in other chapters. Each of the core principles is explored in detail in the subsequent text. These are principles for the coach to work by and with, for the team leader, and for members to apply, as they seek to be that high-performing and sustainable team. Like so many things in life, they come from personal experiences which my colleagues and I have had over the last 20 years in coaching teams, and are borrowed, creatively interpreted and refined in order to be useful for our own practice as coaches as well as the leaders and teams we serve.

1. All things are connected

If you want to create different team results you not only have to act differently as a team, but the situation often requires a shift in the way you as team members think and feel about yourselves and what you assume about yourself, others and your task. Who you are determines what you do, which determines what you get.

A useful way of thinking about this is the connection between what we have in our lives and the actions that we took to acquire those things. We may, for instance, have a nice house, nice car and a loving family. If we stop to think about the actions that we took to be surrounded by these things, then we might rest on having worked hard at university, or school, having met the right people to get a good job, chosen a location in the world that meant that we could meet the right partner and start that lovely family. The quality of those choices to work hard, and to engage with the world around us, is a function of who we are, the content of our character, and what we see as our purpose in life. Figure 3.1 brings this to life.

Who we are has a fundamental impact upon what we do and how we do it and also what we get as a result. The degree of impact and the connection between these things is also a function of the context within which we operate, including the values of the society in which we live. But if we put those things to one side for a second, it is easy to see that who we are and how we show up (our sense of being) does impact what we do and what we get. To put it in more business-related language, values and beliefs (being) lead to actions (doing) lead to results (having).

Figure 3.1 Being, Doing, Having

The more we can continue to make those connections and understand the relationships between them, the more we will see real learning and real change in ourselves occur. The proposition that all things are connected is also one for organizations as a whole. We will talk more about this later in this chapter as well as in the chapter specifically on 'systems'.

Useful questions: Within you, and within your organization, what are you getting and is that what you want? What needs to be more connected?

2. Slow down to speed up

To take advantage of the opportunities to learn, you need to slow down. This allows assumptions to be explored and challenged and ultimately leads to a better quality of decision and action.

This principle has a lot of resonance for our clients who are consistently operating at high speed, seeking to get a lot of things done in a short amount of time. And yet slowing down when the pace is high requires a lot of faith that the time used will be valuable. It is interesting talking to senior leaders and teams about their response to the COVID-19 pandemic. Early on in the crisis many teams cut their roster of activities, refocused on a small number of simple goals and redistributed team members and tasks. This was all done at high speed, initiating a fast response to significant external threat. There came a point with all the teams that we have spoken to however, that slowing down long enough to understand what was happening and being learnt was the order of the day. In fact, the best teams we have worked with over the last 20 years set aside time to learn about how they can expand their capacity to deliver and to lead ever more effectively.

In a sense, this is what an external coach consistently helps a team do by setting aside time to focus on important conversations. And those conversations are about task as well as developing relationships. All of them, however, can contribute significantly to alignment of team members. If the team is not aligned, team members will end up in very different places in a very short amount of time. You will waste resource and you will lose opportunity – think of a team crossing the Antarctic – they may each only have a 0.5° bearing difference between them, but after a few miles they will be some distance apart.

This idea of slowing down to speed up to gain alignment (among other benefits) is most neatly encapsulated in the learning cycle, first created by the psychologist Kolb in the 1980s. It is a depiction of what happens automatically in order that we learn how to respond to our environment – we don't think about it, but it happens. And the version of the cycle we use comes from Peter Senge at MIT. The cycle has four principal elements. The first two are that you engage in action, then reflect on what you've done. The third is that you make some connections between what you wanted and what you've got, between the people involved and between the different ideas about what might now be necessary. Then you move to the final stage where you decide what to do next.

Figure 3.2 The Learning Cycle
(Adapted from Senge et al. 1994)

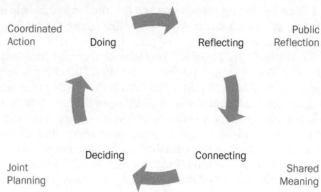

| Coordinated Action | Doing | | Reflecting | Public Reflection |

Joint Planning — Deciding — Connecting — Shared Meaning

Useful questions: Where do you spend most of your time? What might you change for you and your team?

When we use the learning cycle with senior leadership teams, both in ordinary as well as extraordinary times, we invite them to share where they spend most of their time and (appropriately) most say on the left-hand side: 'we decide, and we do'. Some say they do reflect, which is helpful, but the vast majority say that they do not do enough connecting, and this is despite the fact that they know that being clear and aligned on things like their purpose and their goal set is critical. There has been a lot written about the importance of common goals and a shared vision. You only get that if team members are all looking at the same thing and *meaning* the same thing. You only get that shared meaning and therefore alignment if you slow down long enough to have those important conversations. Move too quickly and you go to decision-making with only half the story.

It is useful to reflect on how we prefer to learn – each team member will have their own preferences. However, in our experience this model is incredibly useful in shining a light on collective behaviour and our propensity to miss opportunities to be truly aligned and make high-quality decisions that translate themselves into coordinated action.

Vignette: Some time ago we carried out a study of an oil and gas asset leadership team looking after old assets in the North Sea. They had sought to fix a 'wicked problem' (one that kept on returning) a number of times and it had not worked. So, a performance coach who was supporting the team gathered them together and invited them to spend time understanding the real nature of the problem that they were trying to solve. Over a period of two days, they had slowed down sufficiently to have uncovered some show-stopping assumptions about what the real problem was, established ways of testing different solutions and had aligned on their collective approach. They left with complete alignment on the way forward. Following that session, they did resolve the problem rapidly and the team cited that session as making a material difference to asset performance.

3. It's loops, not lines

No change is linear, all change is in loops and it is the loops that help you learn from experience. Life is not linear – it is more like snakes and ladders than a predictable train journey.

Back in the 1990s, Chris Argyris, Professor at Harvard Business School, wrote a *Harvard Business Review* article entitled 'Teaching smart people how to learn' (Argyris 1991). In it he wrote about the challenge of learning in modern organizations, and particularly challenges that leaders face in initiating and leading change. His basic proposition is that organizations need to continue to learn and indeed to talk a good game about that imperative. In addition, he highlighted what he described as the 'learning dilemma' – that, although important, organizations find it incredibly difficult, and don't even admit to or are really aware of that difficulty. He talks about the narrow definition of learning being on 'problem-solving', on 'fixing things in the external environment'. He terms this 'single loop learning'. At that time, his research told him that 'highly skilled professionals are frequently very good at single loop learning' (Argyris 1991, 4) but less good at what he termed 'double loop learning'. This idea to me is quite profound. In double loop learning leaders are invited to explore their own behaviour and the drivers for that behaviour in order that they can be part of the change that they are seeking to create. If one is able to do this – to operate both at the single and double loop learning levels, one avoids the trap of becoming irritated, frustrated, defensive and embarrassed that you can't lead change or initiate or sustain it by yourself. Or by continuing to behave in a consistent manner without changing when you meet resistance. This requires, in senior leaders, and, of course, when they are together, in their teams, to bring a fair degree of self-awareness, individually and collectively. It also requires a bit of courage – to be able to deal with the embarrassment, the prospect of failure or the requirement that you need to change in order that others can do so. It requires an assessment of what you do truly value, and the degree to which you might be lying to yourself, or not truly hearing others and empathizing with their views.

So, the first idea contained within 'it's loops, not lines' is that this process of examining and learning is not just at a single but a double loop level. The second idea is that change is not linear. The classic idea of success being represented on a graph where the line moves steadily from bottom left to top right, is an illusion. Although we intellectually get the idea that one needs to continue to learn, we struggle with the self-examination that is required in order to be able to effect that learning over time. Over many years of working with teams, I have come to the conclusion that team success looks more like snakes and ladders than a neat graph from an MBA programme.

Useful question: If the 'it's loops, not lines' principle were used in your organization, what would you be doing differently?

Figure 3.3 Snakes and Ladders anyone?

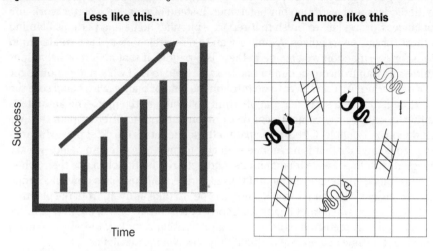

Less like this...

Success

Time

And more like this

4. Be aware of rackets

It is part of the human condition that we sometimes declare intentions that we do not follow through on. These 'rackets' can seriously impede an organization's progress. Rackets is a concept that is borrowed from transactional analysis (Stewart and Joines 2012). It is both a concept as well as when translated into practice a powerful tool in the process of change. Those of you who are familiar with the work of the social psychologist Kurt Lewin (1951) will know that for any change to occur the forces driving the change forward need to be greater than those holding it back (this is where we get the Force Field Analysis beloved of consultants). The forces holding it back can be divided into those that are external, as well as those that are internal to the subject – people. One of the most challenging forces holding change back is what Chris Argyris would describe as 'predictable dishonesty'. This phrase seems to strike a chord with many of our clients who even before the explanation of the phrase, know what we are talking about.

All of us have made commitments that we have found it difficult to deliver on for one reason or another. Examples include getting fit, losing weight, having a better work–life balance, writing a book! Leaving aside the idea that procrastination is a powerful force in many of our lives, we can turn these blockages around by examining the potential internal and psychological 'racket' (or wilful/subconscious self-deception) that we are involved in. The term racket is borrowed from the racketeers in America in the 1930s who ran speakeasies, where the shop front gave a very different impression to the activity being conducted behind closed doors.

The difference here is, of course, that the racket is something going on inside us – a racket therefore is behaviour that takes us away from the commitments that we make. Instead of going to the gym we end up on the sofa, eating crisps and justifying our behaviour. Instead of creating a better work–life balance, we stay late to finish that report – phoning home and perhaps blaming others for our own choices. A simple way to move this forward is to understand that for every action we engage in there is a payoff. If that action or behaviour takes us away from our commitment, then we need to find what that payoff is for not delivering. We don't have to go through the pain of our muscles being sore the next day, maybe a sufficient payoff from not going to the gym. The antidote is either to change the commitment or to recommit with a different plan that we find more actionable. Often, anticipating these rackets is the most powerful antidote to behaviour that is not in line with commitments. As human beings we are blessed with impressive imaginations, and yet are taught not to use them when we are thinking about creating a different future. Psychologists now encourage us to consider what might stop us, not in order to take us away from the pull that we experience when thinking about improvement but to anticipate and plan for us engaging in predictable dishonesty and creating a racket, thereby spending much of our time and energy on justifying our own intransigence.

It is good to bear in mind that we all have rackets, and that they may give us short-term benefits, *but* we pay the costs later. Leaders who fail to notice rackets lose their ability to enrol others, yet leaders who notice their rackets gain the choice to unlock their power as enrollers. And when team members become aware of their rackets as a team, that team gets stronger and better able to address its challenges.

A rackets exercise

Here is an exercise we use with leaders, teams and with multiple teams when they come together to learn and create change together.

Background: The 'racket' is a name for a pattern of behaviour that can weaken us at three levels: as a person, as a team and as an organization. Looking at our rackets gives us choices as leaders to strengthen our impact.

Purpose: To become aware of rackets that can pull you away from your leadership and how to bring yourself back; and address organizational rackets that can weaken a team or organization.

Process: Select a commitment in the team that you are struggling to deliver.

1 What is your commitment?
2 What is your racket (i.e. the behaviour that takes you away from this commitment)?
3 What benefit or pay-off does the racket give you?
4 What does your racket cost you, in the short term and longer term?
5 What can and will you do?

For that final question, you have a choice: to redefine it or, often more importantly, to let it go and stand accountable to an active choice to NOT do it.

Vignette: In supporting a senior leadership group of 40 to align around their declared intention of building a coaching and performance culture, we asked each group represented in a 'whole system workshop', to share their commitments to the shift in culture. We then asked them to share the behaviours that ran counter to that declared commitment and the benefit of continuing to engage in those behaviours together. The discomfort they displayed turned to forthrightness as they opened a conversation about what was really required and how they could support each other. It was a powerful moment that stemmed from confronting organizational rackets.

5. Be on purpose

True interdependence and unity behind a team's purpose will help team members identify with the team as a place to invest their efforts, above other teams they are part of. This strengthens the effectiveness of the team's actions.

There has been much written and talked about on the subject of finding purpose. From Victor Frankl's *Man's Search for Meaning* (1946) to the importance now placed on meaningful work for well-being and flourishing (Seligman 2011), it is crucial that team members engage with the team's purpose in a way that they find meaningful and indeed that the purpose of the team strikes them as a meaningful one. We shall talk more about purpose at a later date, but this has both an existential tug – what is my purpose on this planet? – as well as a practical one – what are we here to deliver and what is our particular contribution to the outcomes of the organization? This principle of being 'on purpose' also implies for us an alignment once agreement has been made.

There is also a message here for the coach, beyond the fact that helping a team articulate its purpose is important. That message is that being clear on one's purpose as a coach is important. This may seem obvious, but just as with a team, there are competing purposes that one might have – to play safe, to shake the team up a bit, to understand, and so on . . . so being clear is important for the coach because so much can then flow from that clarity.

Useful Question: How clear, compelling and meaningful is the team's purpose?

6. Other realities are available

It is seductive to consider our own views as the only reality. Keeping open to the very idea that other realities exist and are equally valid allows greater collaboration, better decision-making and more creative problem-solving.

One of my colleagues runs her own business, which she has named 'Middleground'. She created the name by reflecting on the work that she did with her clients. The more that she thought about it, the more that she felt that by bringing different parts of the system, and different team members together, the more she was creating a 'middle ground'. With this came the opportunity for compromise or, when the task was great, for true collaboration. The process whereby this occurs, often starts by inviting different parties to declare what they are focusing their attention on and what they're noticing about that. If everybody does that, then it is quite easy to see why an impasse might have been reached, or why it has been tricky to solve a problem or come to agreement. Also, it is easy to see that different realities are available.

The phrase 'different realities are available' was coined by a brilliant client through our discussions with the executive team – it was not long before everybody in the business had 'other realities are available' as their screensaver. This was triggered in a conversation focused on their leadership team needing to see their own situation and that of the business in a different way in order to unlock future possibilities. Another way of saying this is that things are how you see them. My son is a student of philosophy. We have fascinating conversations about the nature of reality – particularly now in this political climate. And yet at a basic level he would agree with me that a chair is a chair partly because of its function not just its name. 'Chair' has a particular meaning for us. Language translates quite quickly into assumptions and meaning. We need to tread with caution so that we can make sure that we, as my colleague would say, 'can hold our assumptions lightly' knowing they are not fixed.

A very useful tool in this regard is Chris Argyris' Ladder of Inference – certainly in our own work it allows us to unpick some of the more intransigent assumptions that we make. The proposition is that from one observation one can quite quickly climb a 'ladder', inferring assumptions that drive intentions and then action. All of this happens very quickly, and often we are not aware of it at all. If we slow down a bit, we can realize that that one thing that we observed can be seen from a number of different angles and if done, especially with others, we can draw different and more helpful conclusions.

Useful questions: Select a team challenge. What are the top five ways in which one might see the challenge? Which is most useful?

7. Locate and nurture what's working

Switching from fixing things to locating excellent practice energizes and helps the team (and those the team leads) learn and learn more quickly, breaking down silos as sharing increases.

This idea is taken from the discipline called Appreciative Inquiry (AI). It has its own set of principles and assumptions, as we are laying out ours here. This particular principle, however, also has its roots in positive psychology. We are very familiar with what I would describe as the medical model of diagnosing a problem and finding a solution. This simple gap analysis is at the heart of much of organizational practice. And yet it misses the opportunity provided by finding out where things are already working well and understanding how those areas of good practice and success can be replicated. Building upon what works releases a 'growth mindset' (Dweck 2012) and allows the team to see that life is not all about fixing things, which often turns out to be a whack-a-mole strategy, but that their work is much more about nurturing the good, building upon it, and creating a foundation in which everybody sees what is working well and expands it.

The pedigree of this idea – mainly positive psychology – is now extensive and part of the psychologist's lexicon. Perhaps the most important contribution, and an early one, was made by Barbara Fredrickson and her Broaden and Build theory (2004). The theory, widely supported by the science, is that 'positive emotions: (i) broaden people's attention and thinking; (ii) undo lingering negative emotional arousal; (iii) fuel psychological resilience; (iv) build consequential personal resources; (v) trigger upward spirals towards greater well-being in the future; and (vi) seed human flourishing' (Fredrickson 2004, 1375). Martin Seligman, the father of positive psychology, himself a clinical psychologist, has, of course, made a huge contribution in shifting our thinking to prize the positive and has shown both in a clinical and non-clinical setting, it has a better chance of being effective.

Useful questions: What is going well in your team and what did the team do to make that happen? Where else could you apply those ideas in the team?

8. We are all systems leaders

Gone are the days when leaders were in control – if they ever were. The modern leader, and therefore the modern team and its team members, must operate as leaders of systems, influencing and engaging others in their quest both within, across and at times beyond organizational boundaries.

We will talk more about systems in the next chapter, and the idea that modern leadership requires you to look at the world and understand the patterns that the individual parts create. When I go to see my osteopath, she is at pains to point out that all things are indeed connected. That the pain that I have going across my right shin is a function of a pinched nerve in my lower spine and the tightness in my psoas muscle that goes across my bottom. The solution, of course, is not just to work on those areas but to take a holistic view of all of the elements that go to make up my daily physical habits – not forgetting that, of course, we concentrate our emotional energy in different parts of our body too. The same is true of organizations – one part affects the other and yet seems to be disconnected from it. It's only when you stand back and look at the whole you realize the relationships between the parts and therefore how you can lead, and lead change effectively. In a later chapter we shall see that this goes beyond simple stakeholder management and towards a deeper understanding of how the whole 'organism' works, and indeed how it is affected by its environment.

Useful questions: What in your organization is not connected that needs to be connected? What will you do about that?

9. Enrol others for lasting change

Many years ago, I came across the idea that as a leader, we need to take a stand. A 'stand' is best thought of as a change you feel deeply about making and rooted in what you see as important and valued by others, though it may be challenging for some. If you are 'taking a stand' to create change, being able to enrol others in that change is critical. Asking good questions and listening well are your greatest assets in truly engaging colleagues in your compelling ideas.

The days of Taylorism at the Ford factories, where managers made decisions based on the work of time-and-motion-study consultants with clipboards and stopwatches, are clearly gone. And thank goodness, too. However, when modern organizations embark on a change programme, they often make the mistake of assuming that the world is an entirely rational place, and if there is a good plan with a series of milestones and a logic to the outcome that is required, change will be easy. Economists have for a long time now realized that their basic assumption that people act rationally, is not sustainable. The same is true of organizational change. People act always with a purpose in mind, even if they are not aware of it. Their expressions are a combination of the rational, emotional and the social. By this I mean there is some logic, always, there is an emotional driver behind this, and their utterances say something about the social system of which they are a part. Seeing that makes it a bit easier to realize why truly enrolling others, where enrolment is about getting alongside, understanding, and aligning aspirations, with change imperatives is the way to go. Again, this requires leaders and teams who are initiating or leading change to be good at enrolling others. Good at both the rational as well as the emotional component involved in enrolling. Without enrolling others, change will fail. However good the rationale is for that change.

Useful question: What do you want to change in your team and who else can help you make that happen?

10. Remember rule No. 6

I have borrowed rule No. 6 from Ben Zander. Former conductor of the Boston Philharmonic, he is an inspirational leader and with his wife wrote a book about his leadership philosophy called the *Art of Possibility*. This chapter has a twinkle in its eye in the same way that the author does. Rule No. 6 is actually 'Don't take yourself so goddam seriously'. Coaching teams and working in them is a serious business. But it should also be fun.

Useful question: How can you enjoy being with your team today?

Summary

The 10 core principles of the truly Adaptable Team will help you and the teams that you work in and alongside to be more effective.

Those core principles are:

- All things are connected.
- Slow down to speed up.
- It's loops, not lines.
- Be aware of rackets.
- Be on purpose.
- Other realities are available.
- Locate and nurture what's working.
- We are all systems leaders.
- Enrol others for lasting change.
- Remember rule No. 6.

4 Before you start coaching the team

Start before you start

There is an old consultancy adage that the intervention starts with first contact with the client. They will be affected by how you show up, the questions you pose and the quality of your listening. The same is true, I would argue, of a newly appointed team leader. Pay attention to beginnings. Really understanding the team and its current situation and context as well as its strengths and aspirations and carrying yourself in such a way that team members can more readily 'make real' their most valuable contribution is invaluable work. So 'slow down to speed up'.

In this chapter, we lay out the preliminary questions relevant to a thorough and 'collaborative' understanding of the team and its context. This section is helpful to the team coach in their preparations to support the team, and for the leader who can assess the team's current state and choices that they and the team have. The same questions remain relevant for the team's ongoing performance and learning.

Initial understanding

Before starting to coach the Adaptable Team

Before embarking upon its journey, it is important for the coach and the leader to understand what the team has working in its favour, and what is in their collective favour too – as Hamlet had it '. . . the readiness is all . . .' (*Hamlet*, Act 5, Scene 2). This will avoid a lot of pain for all. Here, we look at the external and internal factors that are useful to consider in coaching teams. There are some really useful questions to be posed up front and should there be an opportunity to develop a coaching plan, the answers can be taken into account in the contracting and then the design process. This can assist the team leader to understand how best to prepare the team for its work together or team coach how best to support the leader and the team. In addition, this process of reflection and planning can assist the coach and the leader to understand the team's task, the relational requirements, as well as its context and the multiplicity of systems that the team is required to serve.

We recommend that coach and team leader, or if you, the team leader, are coaching the team, then with a trusted team member, sit down and discuss the context for the team and these preliminary questions. Once done, a judgement can be made as to how to proceed. The questions at the end of the chapter can be used by a coach to provide a snapshot of the team's current state.

'To team or not to team, that is the question . . .'

It doesn't quite have the poetic moment of the original, but this question, 'Do we need to be a "team" or not?' is still asked quite a lot. As Hamlet continues, is it worth 'taking arms against a sea of troubles and by opposing, end them?' and one might continue . . . 'is it really worth the pain?' While the organizational structure may dictate that team members are all part of the same 'unit', and the configuration has logic, still the question remains – do they actually need to do anything together? And is it worth the effort trying to get really good at it? It would be a pretty impressive bit of organizational planning if you were expected to come together with your colleagues without any purpose at all, but some teams feel like that has happened to them. As a result, the meetings are a morass of heart-sinkingly grim conversations, endlessly padded out with one-to-one reporting. Team members become spectators at the Colosseum, as the boss gives the thumbs down to their colleagues. The question 'do we need to be a team?' is not a very useful one. It is binary, demanding a team/no team response.

Questions that are more helpful

There are two much better and more practical questions:

1 **What are you trying to *achieve* together?**
2 Then, the follow-up question is **'Where do the 'team' members need to work together effectively to achieve that?'**

From the responses to these questions, decisions can be made as to the extent and nature of the teamwork required. It is a judgement as to how far you go in enhancing the team's capability of course. The interplay between the leader, the team and the task, as well as the context, all have a part to play in that judgement.

If, in responding to these questions, there is really nothing there, and no overt need to work together on any task, don't bother. It may be that a need to get together persists. This is likely to be a need that is related more to relationships. The outcome sought could be about belonging, affiliation, learning, or networking. So, focus on those things. Avoid confusion with a need to progress a task together. Everyone can lighten the load and move on.

Other useful questions that can refine conversations and where to focus team improvement efforts are as follows:

3 **How complex is the team's task in pursuing that outcome?** The more complex, the more it will require team members to collaborate and co-ordinate their activity and align on a common purpose.
4 **How new is the task?** The more novel the task is or the more innovation in decision and action is required, the more a team approach will benefit the outcome.

5 **How demanding is the task of team members' skill and experience?**
The more demanding, the more the team will need to work together.

Further exploration: some specific judgements for the leader

Leading academics Ruth Wageman and colleagues in *Senior Leadership Teams* discuss the four reasons a leader might wish a 'real' leadership team to emerge. Those four are:

- Significant growth or retraction
- Horizontal integration of semi-autonomous units
- Major issues in capital / other resources
- Externally originated challenges to traditional ways of operating.

And Wageman et al. (2008) go on to describe the leadership functions that need, as a result, to be fulfilled collaboratively:

- Information exchange for alignment
- Consultation with the leader of the team on complex strategic decisions
- Co-ordination of a key change or interdependent operations
- Decision-making about critical enterprise issues.

So, if the stakes more generally are high, the likelihood is that they need to be more like a team – the task is too great for one person, or just the leader, to attend to and it will require a lot of co-ordination. There is a palpable requirement to get good at working together quickly. This focuses everyone on the specifics and encourages them to work on those activities that will make the difference.

Considerations of the system you are leading and serving

Other useful questions relate to the organization you are leading or serving.

- **How do you wish the departments/teams below you to work?** If you wish them to collaborate, it is much better to be good at it doing it yourselves first – as Gandhi had it, 'be the change you wish to see in the world'. Like layers of an onion, one part of the system – in this case the departments below a leadership team – will be affected by the leadership team. If they see infighting and competition, they will mirror that behaviour, showing that it has become acceptable, even desirable, as a result of what they have seen in the leadership team. So it is useful to start out with that in mind.
- **How do you wish other stakeholders to experience you?** People talk about the 'shadow of the leader', though I see the shadow of the top team to be pretty long too, affecting staff and customers equally and in different ways. We discuss stakeholders more in the later chapters.

More notes on interdependence: task and goal

What we have been looking at in the questions above relates to an important qualifier for there to be a team at all: the different kinds of interdependence that exist for a team. We define interdependence as 'reliance on one another to complete tasks, reach goals and reap rewards' (Guzzo, Salas and Associates 1995). That definition divides up three different kinds of interdependence – task, goals and rewards. In a sense we have to this point been looking at task and goal interdependence. The more the task and goals demand it, the more you will need to collaborate and require good teamship and the fostering of interdependence within the team.

Task and goal interdependencies can come in two forms: actual interdependency, which is practical, and you can see and touch; and 'felt interdependence'. Actual interdependence is as above – and the definition describes real reliance. Felt interdependence is the feeling that you need to work together to be able to deliver. Both need to be in play. Only one can be delivered through coaching. That one is felt interdependence.

Example of task interdependence: We worked with a leadership team seeking to do a big job in a new organization. We had made the assumption that the team's design was in line with the goals and the tasks they had set and fitted with the, in this case many, stakeholders with whom they were required to work, day to day. And yet they weren't. I must say that that assumption was made by both us as well as the client. By the time it became clear that it was difficult for the team to move forward without change, we had made some progress, but it hit some black ice. We took a pause, the team reorganized itself to be significantly more congruent with the needs of stakeholders and the way that they organized themselves, and the coaching recommenced. It was, as a result, a much more successful team, and our coaching was significantly easier and more productive.

Reward interdependence

Interdependence of reward is more of a 'structural' question. It relates to the organizational reward system. Many organizations these days operate a reward and bonus system based not just on individual delivery, but on collective delivery. Research has shown that reward systems that relate to team effort contribute to superior team performance (Hackman 1987). In addition, not just based on delivery of objectives but also how those objectives were delivered – was there collateral damage, was behaviour consistent with the values of the organization? It is worth exploring the reward structure for the team that you're working with, or if you are a leader considering the impact of the reward structure on immediate team behaviours. Even with individual bonus systems, it is not an insurmountable challenge to go against the incentivized behaviour; however, it does make life more difficult for the team in its work together. The only force that will override that incentive in the longer term is an extremely high commitment to each other and to delivery that team members individually and together find highly meaningful.

From all of this discussion on interdependence, if the team or the team members do not actually need to work together – by design their roles don't overlap or interconnect in any way – then coaching is a futile business.

Composition of the team

It is useful to consider the composition of the team – and look at the team members themselves:

- What skills and abilities do they have?
- What experiences do they bring to the team?
- What personality characteristics do they have?
- And perhaps an additional useful question for the coach: how do they show up?

As a team coach, you would not be able to change any of the above; indeed, as a leader, you may not be able to do so immediately. So, the conversation's purpose will be to inquire, to be curious. Having found out about the tasks and the leader's aspiration, you are now finding out about the team members and how they may match the requirements of the task – and importantly if you are the coach discussing this with the leader, what the leader observes and how they are minded to respond. It is interesting to reflect on the process by which team members are selected, given that 'effective teamwork goes beyond assembling a team of experts with the needed task work skills' (Salas et al. 2005). Selection for team orientation will make it more likely that team members will contribute to 'co-ordination and communication . . . and work towards team goals' (Mohammed and Angell 2004).

Culture of the organization

It is also helpful to know more about the culture that the team is working in. Culture is variously defined as 'a pattern of beliefs and expectations shared by the organization's members. These . . . produce norms and powerfully shape . . . behaviour' (Schwartz and Davis 1981); 'A quality of perceived organisational special-ness' (Bratton and Gold 2012); 'The shared beliefs top managers have about how they should manage themselves and other employees and how they should conduct business' (Lawrence and Lorsch 1986) or simply as 'How things are done around here' (Drennan 1992).

So, the team is surrounded, like a fish in water, by this invisible yet important culture. Understanding the nature of that culture is important.

Example of cultural imperatives: We worked with a leadership team in the utility sector, responsible for IT, including IT to the recently acquired nuclear part of their business. The (reassuring to us) level of control and procedure required in the nuclear site of the operation was substantial and different from the other parts of the operation they served. The external culture of the two organizations coming together was matched in the leadership team, where it was like two teams with two very different ways of doing things, two different standards and different paces of work. Early on, our role was to support the two halves of the team share the cultures they inhabited, and select the best elements of each, inviting them to leave those that did not, behind them. This allowed them to build trust and align on a different future.

So, the softer cultural influences on the team are important to bear in mind. I like the questions below as a guide to what to listen out for – they are provocations really, so less useful to ask directly unless team members feel the team is a safe place to share. They can tell you something about the forces on the team and help the team see the water they are swimming in:

- Can employees break the rules?
- Is the big boss human?
- Can the little person rise to the top?
- Will I get fired?
- Will the organization help me if I have to move?
- How will the boss react to mistakes?
- How will the organization deal with obstacles?
- (From Martin et al. (1983) in Burnes (2004))

More specifically on culture, it is interesting to note the degree to which collaboration and team working is encouraged. Some organizations still retain an individualistic feel even though they talk a good 'team game'. This may well have a material impact upon the nature of the coaching that is going to be most suitable for the team and indeed whether the team coaching will be successful.

Example of culture and collaboration: The leadership team of the back-office function of a finance house became clear on its own picture of success for itself and its contribution to the organization and therefore its purpose. It recast its goals and noticed that there was some support that the team could usefully gain from one of the functions. Representatives of that function came to one of our sessions and were enrolled in a more collaborative relationship – this helped the two functions connect.

Autonomy and latitude of the team to control and influence

In addition to a cultural expectation for collaboration and team working is the degree to which the team has autonomy or the latitude to make decisions and to act on them. A senior team may have governance processes that require certain decisions to be made in certain ways; and if it is a management team further down the organization it may have a carefully crafted decision-making protocol. It is therefore always important to check the boundaries within which the team can and cannot operate.

Example of lack of autonomy: The team of another back-office function in a major charity sought help in, among other things, managing an office move. Little did we know that not only was it fraught with politics, but the team had very little latitude to choose how it managed the move. The leader, who chose not to participate in the conversation, then found it difficult to accept their propositions, and we left the scene. This small intervention told us a lot about the culture of that organization – an organization I chose not to work in again, though from this one event, I learnt much about the practical purpose and process of contracting.

Example of lack of control/influence: We had been working with the direct marketing team of an advertising and marketing agency who worked for the government. The management team of eight had a new leader who was less experienced in leadership and a number two who I had come across before and had a lot of confidence in. The leadership team, as well as the wider direct marketing group of around 20 people, reported experiencing a lot of stress with absenteeism on the rise and two members on sick leave. My initial enquiry and working with the top two leaders to understand what was happening and what conversations they needed, uncovered the reality of the situation – that although their resources could have been managed more effectively and they could work together more effectively as a team, the culture of the organization was very much to get the work done, with very little latitude to adjust the brief or acquire new resources to be able to effect that and meet client need. In a sense, whatever I did as coach could only serve to help them manage the situation where they had, or felt they had, very little latitude or control. Unless they could adjust the amount of throughput or the amount of resources and exert influence over the wider system and the cultural imperatives dominating the organization, they would continue to be challenged. In fact, if any team does not have much autonomy it will be less likely to create a truly effective team.

Interview checklist

Initial interviews with team members

Here is a selection of questions to pose to team members to assist a 'collaborative understanding' of the team. From this you can check assumptions and clarify what is going to help and hinder you and the team, as well as confirm the real needs beyond those overtly presented. In addition, it can help you build relationships with team members such that your ability to challenge them at a later date becomes possible.

It is a semi-structured interview process and is usually timed at around 45 minutes. On occasions it is sufficient to ask four to five simple questions; at other times, you need a greater and more detailed spread of questions. Some questions overlap and the client will answer one question when they are being asked about another. When we use this process, the interviews are confidential in that although quotes will be used, names will not be attributable to the quotes. Once done, we usually put the interviews together, pulling out the key themes and supporting them with quotes. This can then be shared with the leader and then the team as a way of confirming the current state. An alternative is to use this just for your own purpose and design.

Questions for individual team members

You and your own team

> What is your role and how do you experience it?
> How is your own team performing?
> What are the key challenges?

The team

> Who are the team's key stakeholders and what do they require of the team?
> What do stakeholders currently say about performance?
> How would you describe the culture of the organization?

Team performance and learning

> What are the key opportunities and challenges the team faces at this time?
> What are the key strengths for the team at this time?
> What does the team need to learn?
> How would you describe the performance of the team?

Team in more detail

> What is the purpose of the team at this time? (And how clear is that role?)
> What is the vision for the team? (And how clear / compelling is it?) and for the business it leads?
> What are the goals of the team?
> How are decisions made?
> To what degree do team members hold each other accountable for decisions / agreements that are made in the team?
> How would you describe current relationships between team members?
> To what degree do team members support and challenge each other?
> What are the meetings like? (When are they, how long, who leads, their purpose, etc.?)

Outcomes

> What would be a great outcome from this process?
> What does the team need to learn to aid future success?

Summary

- Before beginning to support the team, the team coach and indeed the team leader can usefully collaborate to understand more of what will be working in the team's favour.

- If a team does not have a fair degree of interdependence it will be difficult to support it, through coaching. Interdependence is defined as 'the reliance on one another to complete tasks, reach goals and reap rewards'. In order to understand more about the nature of the interdependence that does exist, understanding what the team is trying to achieve together, how complex, new and demanding the task, is important.
- The team leaders also need to ask themselves what function they wish the team to perform given the nature of the tasks that they have, as well as how they wish the wider enterprise to experience them.
- Consideration of the composition of the team and the culture of the wider organization is also critical to give team coaching the best chance of success.
- It is helpful for the team coach to interview members of the team to find out more and a question bank is offered to support this.

5 Coaching the team

You are the instrument of change

As a team leader who uses their coaching skills to support the team and as a professional team coach, you are the instrument of change. Who you are, the intentions that you have and what you then do with the teams that you support and challenge, is all part of the craft of helping teams to be more successful.

This chapter is for both the professional coach and the leader who uses coaching skills with their team. We look at the purpose of team coaching, the distinctions between team and one-to-one coaching, and the challenges in being a 'helper'. The chapter finishes with the knowledge, skills, abilities and qualities of a team coach to assist their development.

Coaching the team

What is the purpose of team coaching?

This whole book is really about how to coach, lead and support a team and how a team can help itself. Despite the fact that definitions can be dry, and seem academic and theoretical, it's useful to share a proposition for what team coaching is, in order to then be able to go on and describe how to do it, and how to do it well.

A number of years ago however, I gathered with two of my colleagues, Chris Sheepshanks and Mike Munro Turner, so that we could share our take on what team coaching was and how it differed from one-to-one coaching. In preparing for this book and, of course, in sharing thoughts over the last few years, I have made some adjustments to our ideas through habit, practice and reflection on the latest research and writings from colleagues. I've come to the conclusion that the original proposition still stands. We define team coaching as **'challenging and supporting the team to maximize its performance, learning, enjoyment and sense of meaning and purpose in service of the organization or wider system that it leads'**.

There are essentially three foundational component parts to the team coaching process which imply a degree of skill and knowledge on behalf of the coach (see Figure 5.1).

Figure 5.1 Team Coaching

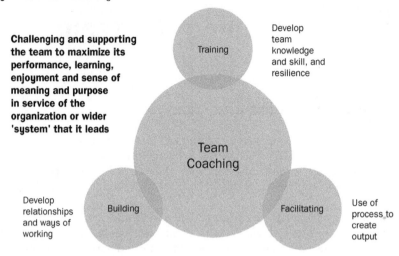

Challenging and supporting the team to maximize its performance, learning, enjoyment and sense of meaning and purpose in service of the organization or wider 'system' that it leads

Training

Develop team knowledge and skill, and resilience

Team Coaching

Develop relationships and ways of working

Building

Facilitating

Use of process to create output

- **Teambuilding.** The purpose of teambuilding is to develop relationships between team members and ways of working such that they will be more successful than they would otherwise have been. Images that come to mind when one thinks of teambuilding are hikes across the moors and trying to build the Eiffel Tower out of spaghetti hoops. Strangely, I think both of these do have a powerful contribution to make to the building of a team – though they are not for everybody. We do occasionally use teambuilding structures and simulation to help a team become more aware of the patterns of behaviour and interaction that might be helping or getting in the way of their ability to deliver. But, often, when they are not used so well those games seem to be the only memory that the team has of having engaged with them rather than the learning that accrues as to how they, in particular, behave either under pressure, in decision-making or in simple interaction with each other. The more one can use these devices in service of challenging and supporting the team the better.

- **Facilitating.** The purpose of facilitation is the use of process to create output. Years ago, I was invited to facilitate an event created in a hurry by a central government department. Conferring with colleagues, I turned the opportunity down as our reflections were that this was a 'poisoned chalice'. There were a number of different suppliers represented in the room and an audience of around 30. The invitation was to facilitate the conversation and agree how the suppliers should all work together. We were to be given five hours to do so. This was most definitely a facilitation job. However, we were one of the suppliers, and had a vested interest in the outcome of the conversations. Second, some of the suppliers were in conflict with each other and with the client. Third, I sensed that the client simply wished to evade responsibility for the outcome, knowing that it was a challenge, and simply wanted somebody to run the process and create a nice neat package with a bow on it at the end of the session. This was not what we did then, nor now. Our purpose in coaching teams was and is to help a team orientate themselves towards an outcome that everybody cares about, and to address the challenging and difficult conversations that would be needed for the team to be successful. We have also worked in 'team to team' situations and between suppliers and client. Despite the fact that we could have facilitated the conversation because that was in our skill set, it was not what we did. We were there to create real conversations, not paper over the cracks. To this day, there is no better distinction I can think of between facilitation and team coaching. Having said that, I know many extraordinarily gifted coaches who describe themselves as facilitators who do exactly what I'm describing to be team coaching. Indeed, one of my go-to books earlier in my career as a coach was *The Complete Facilitator's Handbook* by John Heron (1999), who at that time ran a world-class change programme. So, the definitions are blurred. What's key is that you know what your purpose is, and what conversations you are seeking to create, and you are comfortable you are not papering over the cracks of the team in an effort to maintain harmony – that would be doing the team a dis-service.

- **Team training.** The purpose of team training is to develop the team's knowledge and its skill. Although this may be the outcome of team coaching, it is not the primary purpose of all of the team coaching process. Like teambuilding and facilitating, team training is a very useful device as part of the process, but it is not all of the process. You might, for instance, introduce a listening model to help team members listen to each other prior to an important decision that you then coach the team through. This would develop their knowledge and skill and contribute to a better outcome.

So, team coaching contains training, building and facilitating, but it is not all of those things alone. The 'sweet spot' is when one stands above those and truly challenges and supports the team to maximize their contribution in service to the organization and wider system. The most recent research on the topic of definitions (Jones et al. 2019) concludes that the team coach 'does not provide advice or solutions to the team' and that team coaching is a longer-term process – I would concur and add that when coaching a team, an early structure over time, gives way to an increasingly 'open space' that the coach helps create – and in which the team can take charge of its own learning and performance choices.

As with so many things that are important in life, including work, be it in a small conversation with a direct report, or your role in the team, reflection on your purpose is incredibly important. If you're clear about your purpose as a leader and coach and therefore your intention in any moment, it is much easier to navigate what is in your gift and choice to do, and what is not and therefore the skills that you can bring to bear.

Other elements of team coaching defined

Establishing 'virtuous cycles' of self-regulation

We describe team coaching as an intervention aimed at embedding a **'virtuous cycle'** of team effectiveness into team practice. This idea of a virtuous cycle to us, is incredibly important. As Clive Woodward, the former coach to the England rugby team, may tell you, nothing succeeds like success. Success becomes a habit, one becomes aware of one's vulnerabilities very quickly, and how to adapt and adjust depending on who you're playing and what the context is. The same is true away from sport. The more the team can get into a virtuous cycle with which they are familiar, the more winning becomes habit.

Ensuring sustainability in team performance

In addition, we talk a lot about sustainability. It is easy – or relatively easy – to turn in a good performance once. What's more difficult is to sustain that performance over time. The effort required to get it right once may pay off, but sustainability requires a deeper understanding of what contributed to that initial success. It requires constant learning and attention to be paid to all of the contributing factors that sustain performance, and it requires good leadership at a team and organizational level.

As a result, we would add that effective team coaching enables the team to sustain its output, enhance its ability to perform together in the future and support team members to learn, enjoy and find meaning in their work. It involves raising awareness as to context and choices, challenging the status quo and helping the team to embed team learning in team practice such that the team can 'self-regulate' its way to peak performance.

Individual to team coaching

There are clearly differences between coaching a team and coaching an individual. There are also many similarities. The fundamental skills are, of course, pretty much the same – the ability to contract, to listen effectively, to ask questions that challenge and support, building the relationship over time, and using a number of tools well and at the right time. The team coaching process, however, is more demanding:

- Each individual brings their own differences in personality, experience, skill, values, needs, which can help and seemingly hinder the team coaching process.
- Contracting is more complex given the number of people and the context involved.
- The dynamic of the team is constantly shifting and being able to notice that while attending to one's own team coaching process in support of the team's task can be a challenge.

- Given the need for alignment within the team and between the team and stakeholders in the system beyond the team, the coach needs to support consensus, which can take time. Early on, team members may either not declare their positions or, as events unfold, may hold on to them tightly.
- The leader is in the best position to re-enforce agreements between sessions, though may need support in doing so.

So, there are many more variables in coaching a team than there are in a one-to-one setting and for the team, leader and coach to work with those variables in a measured way is important.

Leader and coach as helper

A leader who is seeking to lead, manage as well as coach their team needs to recognize that they are a helper. All those who are on the periphery, consultants, teachers, doctors, nurses, therapists, psychologists are all helpers too. And being a helper or, should I say, wanting to help, and thinking that you can help, are not sufficient qualifiers to be able to actually help. One needs to think through the dynamic one creates when one steps forward to help others. Psychologists would call this the psychodynamics of the helping relationship.

There is a useful distinction between three different kinds of helper – one is an expert who comes in and provides information or services to help the client understand the situation better. The classic example of this is an old-school consultant who runs a process, runs a study and whose report ends up filed. The second is a doctor, again as an expert, but a slightly different one who is good at diagnosing and prescribing the solution. I would argue that both the expert and the doctor are the ones in control, who have power. The third, what Ed Schein would describe as a process consultant, focuses on building an equitable relationship and clarifies what kind of help is needed, working alongside the client continuously and maintaining equity.

I am here drawing from Ed Schein's book *Helping* (2015), which, despite its compact nature, is a tour de force on this topic of the leader and coach as helper and the psychodynamic relationship between the helper and those being helped. Slightly weirdly when I read the book, I had just had an experience that he uses as an example in the book. I was running for a train, I slipped, and one leg ended up dangling in the gap between the train and the platform. I was left with half of me on the platform and one leg in and one leg out of the train. It was a moment of hideous embarrassment and advancing pain. He uses this as a good example of somebody who manifestly requires help. And yet the crushing embarrassment and loss of status, power and independence, not to say dignity, means that momentarily I, as he describes his victim in the book, am 'down and vulnerable'. Anyone who's seeking to help in that moment is, as Schein describes, 'up and powerful'. Again, in that moment both helper and helpee are uncertain, perhaps even anxious – so that when help is offered it may be briskly rejected. This analogy is, for me, a very helpful one in coaching a client team.

They are asking for help and inviting you to take up your authority – but can you help? And will the team listen to your offer of help?

This is encapsulated neatly in Schein's summary:

- There is an inherent **imbalance of power** in a helping relationship at the beginning.
- The **client is down and vulnerable**.
- The **helper is up and powerful**.
- The **exchange that needs to be affected is unclear** – what will the helper need to do? What will the client need to give up?
- The **implied dependency creates anxiety in both**.
- If this early anxiety is not recognized, both giver and receiver can engage in defensive and dysfunctional behaviour, called 'traps'.

As Schein puts it, 'Helping situations are intrinsically imbalanced and role ambiguous. Socially and emotionally, when you ask for help, you are putting yourself "one down". It is a temporary loss of status and /or self-esteem; it is a loss of independence' (Schein 2015, 31).

Given this imbalance exists to varying degrees at the beginning of the relationship, it's easy to see how the client – be it the team or the leader – can respond in a whole variety of ways. They may say 'thank goodness you can help me I can now turn it over to you', relinquishing responsibility for progressing performance and learning. The team may feel suspicious of your motive, resentful that somebody – perhaps the leader – thinks they need help, and there may even be concealment of the real challenge the team has.

For the coach and leader, the anxiety and implied dependency may tip behaviour towards what Karl Jung described as the 'shadow side'. However capable one might be, it's easy to start acting in a way that if you catch yourself, feels unfamiliar, inappropriate and unskilled.

Healthy interventions and their shadow

Jung first coined the idea of everybody having a shadow side. Lying obscured behind the external face, the shadow side of one's personality is not necessarily wilfully hidden and yet is driven by forces of which we are commonly unaware. They are a distortion of our overt and declared intentions and in a coaching context may stand to damage the relationship or at least impair the ability of that relationship to be a helpful one. Drawing from Egan's work (1998) and adapting it, we can depict the healthy interventions a coach and a team might engage in (on the left of Figure 5.2) and the shadow side (on the right) of that of the coaching process.

Clearly, to guard against the shadow side playing a dominant role – assuming that it will always be there in some form so therefore needs to be managed – one needs to stay aware of oneself, one's emotions, one's moods and reactions, thoughts and feelings. As well as what all of those things are encouraging one to do, and whether they are an appropriate response that will help the team. As a result of that, questions that I find useful for myself as

Figure 5.2 The Healthy and Shadow side of a coaching intervention

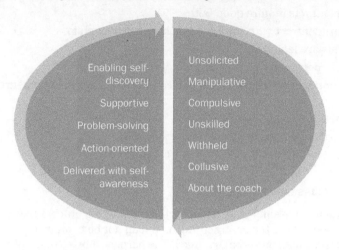

well as indeed for team members when they are managing their own internal shadow of these are:

- What is the situation?
- What am I thinking and feeling?
- What does that make me want to do?
- What might be the consequence of me doing that?
- What do others need from me?
- What do I choose?

Contracting: steering away from traps

The route away from falling into these traps is to strike agreements with your client as to how you will work together. In many ways, these contracts are seen as one-off events, once agreed never to be renegotiated, written down in black-and-white. But in my experience one can only go so far in a written document, however useful that initial understanding may be. As with any relationship it is important to constantly revisit the agreements that have been made both formally as well is informally in order to understand and refresh that agreement, so it is still useful for both parties and indeed equitable and felt to be fair. So, I would encourage everybody who contracts with a team, and the leader of the team, because that is where often the contracting process starts, to see contracting as an ongoing process rather than an one-off event.

It's also useful to remember the words of Peter Block in *Flawless Consulting* (2011) who shared some propositions on contracting:

- The relationship must be 50/50 or it will collapse: you can't get something for nothing.

- Contracts should be freely entered into.
- Good contracts require good faith.
- You can't contract with someone you have not spoken to.
- All wants are legitimate.
- You can contract for behaviour but not feelings.
- Most contracts are broken from neglect, not intent, so writing them down is useful.
- Contracts are always negotiable.
- You can say no to what clients want from you
- (adapted from Peter Block, *Flawless Consulting* (2011)).

A useful process for contracting

It is helpful to have simple headings for the contracting process that cover the principal elements of the contract. Again, it may not be contained in one document and some may be verbally agreed. The purpose, however, is not just to be clear and make the process work, but to lower the attendant anxiety that goes with lack of clarity and that causes dysfunction in the principal relationships.

The headings we have often used are as follows:

Figure 5.3 Contracting

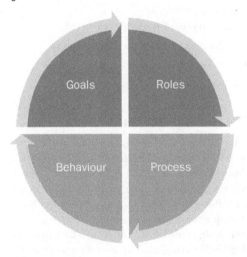

Goals

- Deliverables/outputs
- Outcomes sought
- Measuring success
- What can and cannot be achieved.

Roles

- Roles and responsibilities
- Report/recording/summarizing
- Rights and responsibilities.

Process

- Purpose of the coaching and what the team coach will bring and do
- Contingencies/dependencies
- Confidentiality
- Agreeing on an agenda for the whole process and for the principal parts
- Review sessions for progress checks and mutual learning/feedback
- Completions and endings.

Relationships

- Stakeholders/sponsors
- Behavioural expectations for principal parties.

Once developed with the leader, sharing when appropriate with the team is helpful, so that the team also feels in control of the process and party to the agreements made. It may be that the 'sponsor' is neither in the team nor is that person the leader. It is rare that the sponsor will interfere unduly with the team leader's work, though if they are a board member working with the CEO, engendering collaboration in that relationship is important and could usefully support the team coaching process. It can also assist the coach with understanding more of the dynamic relationships that surround the team.

Knowledge and skills

It is perhaps less fashionable these days to talk about knowledge, abilities and skills when seeking to do something very well. There is something quite useful, not only about knowing things but also being a craftsperson in applying that knowledge. A while ago, I interviewed eight of my colleagues. Each of us had done a substantial amount of team coaching, one way and another, and it was then, as it perhaps remains now, an emerging discipline within the coaching field. The method fell short of being fully scientific, though I used the critical incident process and invited my colleagues to identify one or two teams who they had recently worked with that they felt exemplified team coaching for them. I then invited them to describe the team, their situation and what they did, as well as how they did it. I then drew out the themes from each of those conversations and organized them according to knowledge, ability and skills, and in addition made notes of the qualities that my colleagues reported would be important, and the beliefs that underpinned their practice when working with teams. Since those conversations I've had an opportunity to not only revisit the analysis but build on their experiences as they'd expressed them to draw out both the exterior process of coaching a team and attempt to articulate the interior process of the team coach.

Developing bifocal vision: task and process

Perhaps the most important knowledge, skill and ability is to remember and use the distinction between the team's task – it's overt activity to produce an outcome – and relationships, or as some others call it the team's 'process'. Both task and relationships are consistently running alongside each other, irrespective of which the coach or leader is focusing on, in the team. They are inextricably entwined. Knowing this means that the coach can and needs to develop bifocal vision – being able to understand and see how the task is progressing, as well as how team members are thinking and feeling – about each other, the task, the leader, and the context and wider system. Knowing what you are looking at, at any one moment, while being able to 'process' (make sense of) the other, is a core and fundamental skill, which takes time to acquire, and can be tiring. It is significantly easier therefore if, as is often the case in our practice, there are two coaches in the room to support the team. That means that while both of you may retain dual focus, one can manage the process while the other is processing what is happening between team members. One can then inform the other and ensure the team coaching stays focused and on track.

The body of knowledge: what do you need to know?

Knowledge: 'Organized body of information which, if applied, makes adequate performance possible'

Figure 5.4 Developing bifocal vision

These are the principal headings for the knowledge of a team coach:

- **Teamwork:** A team's developmental journey; how you would know if they were an effective team; stories of other teams
- **Team dynamics:** What it means and how it can be experienced by a team
- **Team leadership:** The principal elements of small team leadership
- **Systems:** Soft systems and constellations, systems thinking
- **Consulting:** A consulting cycle including contracting at the start and throughout
- **Coaching:** The coaches' purpose and role with individual leaders and teams
- **Change:** What change is, how it affects individuals and teams and how that process can be assisted
- **Learning:** How adults learn and how that can be used in a team
- **Goals:** Goal setting and its relevance in a team environment
- **Conflict:** Its sources and impact on team effectiveness; processes for resolution
- **Processes:** A broad range of tools that can be applied in working with teams (e.g. giving feedback)
- **Trust/psychological safety:** The nature of trust/safety and how it is engendered in a team; boundary setting and its importance
- **Ethics:** Adhere to an ethical code (e.g. The British Psychological Society, SGCP) and know how to act in accordance with that code.

In addition, there are some specific tools and techniques that are useful to have in the toolkit or indeed may be the principal 'lens' through which you look at a team and work with them. These will depend on the nature of your work with a team and how you prefer to operate:

- Dialogue: What good conversation is and how it can be encouraged (Bohm 1996)
- Storytelling/Narrative: The process, meaning and use of storytelling in organizations
- Transactional analysis
- Gestalt (Bluckert 2015)
- Psychodynamics for the team and the coach (Beck 2012)
- Sensemaking: How people make sense of their environment (Weick 1995)
- Positive Psychology Coaching (Biswas-Diener and Dean 2010).

Often, a team coach will combine different disciplines and tools and provide an 'integrative' approach, selecting the most appropriate and effective method for the team, while retaining their own principles and world view. The skills and abilities below can then support the coach to be able to use these approaches effectively.

Skills: Capability to perform job operations with ease and precision . . . a performance standard required to be effective

Abilities: Cognitive capabilities necessary to perform a job function . . . requires application of knowledge

There are core interpersonal abilities and skills that are at a premium in a team coaching environment. Given the high number of variables and constantly changing dynamic, each of these core skills needs to be finely tuned.

1 **Listening**
   - Reflecting back accurately what the coach heard the team say or decide
   - Following the team's interest within an agreed agenda/boundary
   - Listening without judgement and exploring meaning in relation to the team's work
   - Summarizing what the team has just said or done and confirming the accuracy of the summary
   - Affirming the team in its expression of feelings and experiences
2 **Giving feedback**
   - To the team from the available data – observations of behaviour and impact on others and the coach
   - Pointing out behaviour and inaction inviting consideration as to its meaning for the team and its work together
   - Sharing possible choices for the team
   - Challenging/confronting behaviour in the team
3 **Asking questions**
   - That generate awareness, choice and responsibility in the team
   - That can challenge and support the team in creating and maintaining momentum
   - Inviting team members to be explicit, to disclose both thoughts and feelings and their implications
4 **Facilitating** the coaching process and conversations in a team towards a goal
   - Being clear on the intent in each intervention with the team
   - Ensuring the conversation is balanced between team members
   - Adjusting the process as required.

Core building blocks of team coaching

1. Building and maintaining relationships

The more that you display trustworthiness (reliability, motives, goal congruence, competence in field), the more the team will allow you to challenge them in service of their work together. This, of course, starts very early on, when you as a coach first meet them, perhaps when you interview each team member in preparation for a team coaching process. We talk more about developing trust within the team in a later chapter, and the lessons there are very helpful for the coach and the leader, as well as for team members. In that initial one-to-one

Figure 5.5 Core Capabilities of Team Coaching

conversation as well as perhaps in an early meeting with the team as a whole, having the team experience you as focused on their agenda, interested in their challenges, and through your questions displaying sensitivity to their context and the demands placed on them is very helpful for your subsequent work with them. You are ensuring that they begin to feel safe in speaking up with you. Ensuring good confidentiality is clearly helpful in that process. In addition, however, ensuring that your expectations of the team and perhaps of them as individuals is also important to be clear. In doing all of these things you are signalling how you wish them to behave towards you. It is an adult exchange. You are engaging in a micro contract with them and establishing boundaries that will support your work with the team as a whole. One additional boundary as the team coaching process unfolds is to know when you have ceased to be useful, or when your process does not appear to be working for whatever reason. Your ability to speak up and invite the team to reflect is, at that point, helpful and reinforces the sense of trust and safety that you will have established early on.

2. Consulting and coaching in context

Determine and articulate the current state and organizational influences and desired outcomes in context.

Determining and articulating, both within your own coaching team and to the client and the team, what you understand about the team and its context is important. An early understanding of all of these things will help your design and help the team, along with you, understand their current state. It is in that sense a 'collaborative understanding', given that they may well not have had an opportunity to view their current state until you had arrived. It is almost certainly true that it will be helpful to have that external assessment derived from conversations with them, all in one place. This opens up the conversation about what needs to be addressed.

3. Designing the team coaching process

Again, early on in the coaching programme there will be design work to understand, clarify and agree with the leader of the team the most appropriate process given the outcomes that are desired. In my experience, designing the team coaching process gets easier as the process unfolds, where the conversations that are required become increasingly obvious. The team is also more able to articulate to you what is needed. At that point, avoiding collusion and retaining the opportunity to challenge their thinking is especially important. For instance, they may seek to focus firmly on task when the lack of progress is down to some order of poor dynamic. The micro skills here are being able to map out a process at a high level, almost like you're having a conversation with the team and are operating as the guide for that conversation; designing the detail of each process – its purpose and how you will run the session, thinking through what you expect to come out and ensuring that you are in good shape to respond appropriately. Creating more detailed coach notes will help the coaching team – the more prepared you are the easier it will be to be flexible in the session. Engaging the client with the proposed outline agendas will ensure that every step means that you're taking them with you.

4. Supporting the team

Create an in-session environment that is 'psychologically safe' and encourages openness and honesty among team members.

We will speak more about psychological safety later on in the book, and what coaches and leaders can do to generate a greater degree of safety. Suffice it to say that your ability as a coach to provide a 'container' for emotions as expressed by the team within the session is important. This includes ensuring that the agreed boundaries of behavioural expectations, even timing of sessions and the like, are retained and referred to, in order to encourage a feeling of safety; inviting team members to tell their stories; have others listen and respond supportively in service of the work the team is doing; and help team members be authentic in their behaviours and in their conversations. It is also useful to be able to spot and share assumptions that are being made in the team that could usefully be challenged, encouraging the team to feel more in control of what is possible.

Through observation of behaviours, theorize on and (where appropriate) share.

As has been described earlier, there is much to attend to and observe when working with the team. It can be quite overwhelming. However, one's ability to observe behaviours and what is said, as well as what is not said, the different physical and conversational positions the team members take up, and the roles that they are playing as well as the language that is being used and any patterns that the team as a whole seem is using, or are caught in, is all invaluable. Being able to theorize on what is happening for the team and how that might be impacting upon their performance, and then being able to share appropriately at the right time is, again, invaluable.

Manage the process of a team session effectively and think creatively under pressure.

The team coach is not just there to 'run the process' – that, as described earlier, is more about facilitation at the very simple end. And yet it will be enormously helpful to the coach if this is something that they do not have to think about too much – it allows them to fully attend to how the team is progressing on its task and with relationships between team members as well as between the team and the systems it serves. Once the plan is in place and you have started the coaching in session, your ability to be fleet of foot and adjust the process as required could well be important. Just as important is knowing when to 'trust the process'. Many times, I have felt that the process is not working and yet the team is simply struggling to have critical conversations together. Opening up that conversation with the team helps you and them.

5. Managing and using self

You are the principal instrument of change in a team coaching process. Knowing what you are thinking and feeling, and what that is encouraging you to do as well as your ability to check whether that's appropriate, is all helpful. Retaining your own boundary – knowing where the team ends and you begin, which are their emotions and which are yours, is also critical. This is not so much objectivity, as being able to accept how things are and know who owns what. Managing your own moods is important, and the kind of energy that will be most effective at different parts of the process is important. As a coach, one can put energy in from the outside or draw that energy from the team. Knowing when to match what you're experiencing and seeing in the team and knowing when to go against it in order to raise the level of challenge is important.

6. Supporting the leader

As has already been described, being able to coach the leader as part of the team coaching is also valuable. The leader plays a critical role in the life of the team, and the relationship between the team and the leader is an important one. It is more difficult for a team coach if the leader in their approach runs counter to, for instance, an atmosphere of psychological safety. Being able to notice and share feedback with the leader as to what they are doing that is both helpful as well as perhaps less helpful to the team, is important. In addition, it is likely that there will be a series of contracting and review conversations throughout the process, which not only build a relationship with the leader but also allow for reflections on their leadership approach and what they might need to change in order to support the team to learn and perform to its best.

Qualities

And finally, some qualities of a team coach that are helpful.
These are a combinations of traits and preferences as well as aspects of 'character'.

- **Clarity** in the coach's role and how that manifests at each part of the process
- **Trust:**
  - In a 'process' – both the overt process as well as the rational and socio-emotional process of making meaning from it
  - In oneself
  - In the team's capacity to learn and perform
- **Courage** to act in an ethical and appropriate manner in service of the team, its outcomes and its growth
- **Presence:**
  - To be fully present and aware of self and others – thoughts, feelings, moods
  - Calmness / not being overwhelmed, being able to observe one's own state while retaining focus on the outcomes
  - Sense of humour – for use with the group and to serve one's own state of mind and that of coaching colleagues
  - Confidence – being able to predict the success of an intervention
  - Managing one's own energy in service of the team
  - Curiosity – an inquiring mind
- **Comfort:** With ambiguity and complexity, seeing them as part of the team's development
- **Empathy:** Being able to step into another's shoes and see the world from their perspective
- **Objectivity:** Working to distinguish fantasy from reality and help the team ground their decisions in reality within a system/context
- **Interest:** In each team member and their learning, performance and well-being
- **Goal orientation:**
  - Focus on objective / purpose / goals
  - Desire to see the team succeed
- **Productive impulse control:** Being able to retain perspective and manage mood in service of the client work
- **Boundary retention:** Appropriate ownership of thoughts and feelings and behaviours.

The four lenses

How to retain multiple perspectives and stay 'clean': the Four Lens Model

The team coaching process can be pretty busy and intense, both within and outside of the sessions with the team. Being able to process what's going on, as has been described above, is very helpful. One can do that both within the session, when you are working with the team, in the moments of downtime that you have within the sessions, as well as away from the sessions. This can be done alone, with a colleague with whom you are working to deliver the team coaching, or indeed with your supervisor. Here we present an approach that can be used in all of those different circumstances, where the purpose is to ensure that you:

- Continue to learn – in the moment as well as over time
- Become emotionally disentangled, and therefore restore your ability to function effectively as a team coach
- Check the quality of your work both from a practical and ethical standpoint.

From bifocals to varifocals

Borrowing from Hawkins and Smith (2013), we developed the four lenses, and present them here so that you can:

1 Manage your own internal process, generating self-awareness and creating options for future action.
2 Support a colleague with whom you are working with in order that you can both decide how to respond to events as they unfold.
3 Follow it as a learning map to brief your own coaching team after part or all of the team coaching process, to generate learning, performance and restoration.

The four lenses

We call them the four lenses because it's useful to focus one's attention on different parts of the system at different times, to be able to understand what is going on and what needs to happen next. For each 'lens', of course, there is a conscious level – those things of which we are aware, that we know are happening and may be rational or irrational to us. In addition, there are unconscious dynamics and forces at play, which we cannot see and can only be known through exploration, using the known as an entry point to understand what is really going on and what is driving conscious action and activity.

Here, we share each of the lenses and a brief description of what falls inside the 'spotlight' as well as some useful questions which may be posed to unlock both conscious as well as the unconscious dynamic.

Figure 5.6 The Four Lenses
(Webster & Firman 2020)

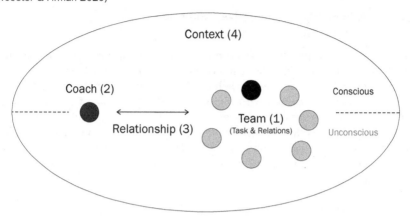

1. Lens one: the team

The focus is on the team's situation – the questions/outcomes the team wants support with, how they present the issues and the choices that they are making. **Questions:** What did you notice about the team? How would you describe their reaction to the task? How would you describe their relationships? What patterns of behaviour are you becoming aware of? Where is their energy and what tells you that? Who is leading and following, challenging and looking on? What theories do you have about the team?

2. Lens two: the coach and the coach's interventions

The focus is on the coach's own experience as an instrument for registering what is happening beneath the surface of the team 'system'. **Questions:** What did you/the coach do? What was your intention? How did you make your intervention(s)? What was the impact? Is there anything that you would change? What do you now want to do with the client? What feedback, if any, have you given to the team? **And:** What do you feel/think about this team? What do you find most difficult about this team? What is your hypothesis about your work with this team?

3. Lens three: the coach–team relationship

This treats the relationship between the coach and the team as a third party, something that is co-created and therefore has a life of its own. **Questions:** What is the quality of the relationship? What is a metaphor for the relationship? Who are you to the client? Who is the team to you? How would you describe your relationship to the leader/particular team members? How is that helping/hindering your work with the team?

4. Lens four: context

The focus is on the wider organizational, social, cultural, ethical and contractual context within which the coaching is taking place. **Questions:** What is going on in the wider system? Who are the key players/stakeholders? What is their relationship to your team? What pressures/freedoms are evident to you? What are the other forces at play that the team is or is not aware of?

Summary

- The purpose of team coaching is to challenge and support the team to maximize their performance, learning, enjoyment and sense of meaning and purpose in service of the organization or wider system that it leads.
- The three fundamental building blocks as a team coach are teambuilding, facilitating and training.
- The team coach is focused on enabling the team to sustain its output, enhance its ability to perform together in the future and support team members to learn, to enjoy and find meaning in their work. It involves raising awareness as to context and choices, challenging the status quo and helping the team to embed team learning in team practice such that the team can self-regulate its way to peak performance.
- When coaching, the leader or the coach is a helper, and as such needs to be aware of the inherent imbalances early on in the relationship with the team. Contracting is an essential part of ensuring that those imbalances are managed well.
- Beyond the base level of coaching skill required to coach a team there is a body of knowledge to examine and perhaps to choose from to build your toolkit as a coach and your own approach. The skills and abilities required are as follows:
  - Building and maintaining relationships
  - Consulting in context
  - Managing and using self
  - Supporting the team
  - Supporting the leader
- Critical qualities such as trust, courage, presence and empathy are all essential for team coaching.
- To be able to learn, restore and maintain good quality, we recommend a supervision process that one can use both within the team coaching session as well as beyond it, by yourself and with colleagues.

6 Systems and stakeholders

We are all connected

It is manifestly obvious that we are all connected. It is true for all human beings on this planet irrespective of who we are, where we are, which country, county, village we call home, or which organizations employ us. There is no escaping the reality that what we do affects others. In the microcosm of our universe that are the teams to which we belong, it is time that we started acting in accordance with this reality.

In this chapter, the importance of systems work in teams (Tate 2009; Hawkins 2011; Leary-Joyce and Lines 2018) is explained and we look at how that works in practice with a team; we examine systems in VUCA or highly changeable environments. In the last five years, it has been a joy to work with a leading exponent of the systems approach, Elana Friedman, and also Chris Sheepshanks, a highly experienced executive and team coach. Both are colleagues at the Centre for Teams, and we discussed systems in the current context. That conversation runs through what follows.

Using a systems lens

What do we mean by systems work in organizations or taking a systems view?

Elana's example – taking a systems approach: I was doing some work on youth crime. In youth offending teams then there was a narrow focus on young people offending and the solution appeared to be a linear one – put more money into youth offending institutions. But the key question was 'How do we stop them offending?' Either you can put them in youth offending institutions or you can widen the lens to examine the system. This is what we did. What else is happening here? We looked at youth services and review services, at what's happening for parents – what kind of support exists for them by way of training or emotional support; at what's happening in the community whether the community structures are breaking down, and you realise that young people beginning to feel that they don't have anywhere to go. If the parks are not being maintained, health services are not being maintained, and the relationship with the police is poor . . . So, in order to solve the crime issue with young people, you actually need to a hold a wider lens, which enables you to see where best to put resources. It may therefore not be in youth offending institutions but in parental support. Breakfast clubs came in as a result of taking a systems lens – children can't learn if they haven't been fed at home, so if we feed them at school, they are more likely to learn.

Systems work is about taking a holistic approach to working with organizations. It's about seeing organizations as human social systems. The more that team members are able to see their team and their organization as systems, the better. It's about stepping out of the forest and starting to see not only the trees but the whole forest. If we can do that, we are able to notice patterns emerging, and to know what's happening much more easily. If you can see the whole of the organization and the interaction of the parts then you can see the flows of information and relationships, what creates them as well as what holds them back, and what the impact is. You can also see what creates balance and where the stress in the system lies. It's about raising your eyes out of your part and seeing the whole.

What is a system?

In *Dance of Change* (2014, 137) Senge et al. define a system as

> anything that takes its integrity and form from the ongoing interaction of its parts. Companies, nations, families, bodies, televisions sets, personalities, and atoms are all systems. Systems are defined by the fact that their elements have a common purpose and behave in common ways, precisely because they are interrelated towards that purpose.

What assumptions do we make about systems?

As with our principles in an earlier chapter, the assumptions we make about systems drive how we use them. Here are some useful assumptions about systems:

- Systems consciously or unconsciously are working to a purpose even if that purpose is unclear.
- There are boundaries we can define to know who is in and who is out.
- There are multiple realities and different things can be happening at the same time.
- There are assumptions even if we don't know what they are.
- The system is playing to a set of rules even if we are not conscious of them.
- There are patterns even if they are unseen.
- There are parts and relationships that bring balance and equilibrium to the system and others that de-stabilize the system – and they are always changing.
- Some parts have more influence than other parts.

This can be brought to life with 'The Systems Game'.

Purpose: to simulate how a system works and learn why a systems perspective is useful to us.

Process: Round 1

- All team members stand in a circle.
- Each team member chooses two people but doesn't tell anyone who they have chosen.
- There are two rules to adhere to: the exercise must be done in silence; each team member must remain equidistant to their two selected colleagues.
- (So, if their people move, then they move; when they are equidistant, they stand still).
- 'Go'.
- **Debrief:** what did the team notice? Team discussion and connections to systems principles and how that relates to their work together.

Process: Round 2

- Coach moves two team members while others remain in place.
- One team member may be asked to watch standing on a chair (taking a 'helicopter' view).
- 'Go'.
- Team moves in silence.
- **Debrief:** What did the team notice? What of the team member on the chair? The more the team can share their experience in the exercise, the easier it will be to connect that with their organization when that is addressed directly.

What kinds of parts constitute a system?

This depends on scale. Different teams can constitute the different parts; different departments can constitute parts; the global organization, the different countries or regions will constitute parts; it can also be a supply chain and looking beyond your organization to the parts of that supply chain. Your clients or customers and suppliers are also parts. The key question is: how big/wide do you want to be looking?

What is the real benefit of using the systems lens and working in this way for coaches and teams?

If we are wanting to solve wicked problems or meet really big challenges, the likelihood is that there won't be just one reason why you are stuck or one opportunity to be seen. There will be lots of parts involved, multiple reasons for the 'stuckness' and many different opportunities to be elicited. So, the more we are able to widen our field of vision and see the myriad of possibilities of what can be influencing the whole and the strength of the challenge, the more insight we are able to bring to it. This allows us to anchor our resources where they need to be – our money, our energy – in a way that then creates a real shift.

Are we looking for 'cause and effect' or patterns?

It's not an 'either or'. 'Cause and effect' is part of it, but it is also 'patterns'. We often talk about 'taking a step back' to a clearer view, and this is what we are doing. Actually, what we think is more powerful is 'taking a step up' – a helicopter view – that's really interesting. It's also about attitude, being more curious: what's happening in the organization? Where are things emerging? How are things emerging? What might be the different causes? What else could be happening? Two of the core questions that are often asked when doing systems work are: 'tell me more' and 'what else?' The more we are able as leaders to become curious at the multiple things that could be happening, the more we open up our minds to see more of the system. We can then start seeing greater patterning.

Stakeholders and systems – are they the same?

Stakeholders are parts of a system and our definition of system may go wider. Staff are stakeholders, as are customers, the CEO, functional departments, governments, parents, schools, even ideas can be parts – for instance, the cultural history of an organization or what might be described as artefacts. So stakeholders are prime, though be on the look-out for more intangible elements that are part of the system.

Exercise 1 for teams in systems: the team and the organization 'in the mind'

The purpose of both versions of this exercise is for teams to express and discuss how they each experience the system of which they are a part. There are two methods:

1. Use of metaphor

We all have a picture in our heads of the organization, our place in it and how we see it functioning. This can come in the form of a metaphor for the organization – a picture to which we give meaning, and that helps us understand how we feel and what we think being in that system and describe those experiences to others. Other team members may have very different pictures of the organization in mind.

We can literally draw or select an image of how we see the organization. For instance, 'I see it as a ship slowly sailing on a calm sea'; 'I see it as being a collection of individuals who are spread out across the page'. This then gives a very interesting narrative. The story that I hold in each, creates assumptions that will influence the way in which I engage with the organization. If I see us all sailing on a boat together and calm seas, the way in which I approach things will be different to seeing it as a group of individuals who are spread out all over the page. Imagery enables us to get a sense of how different people are seeing the organization and how they can start to have a different conversation for greater alignment.

2. Mapping the system

Mapping the system gives us a sense of relationship, distance and direction – it's very powerful to help us notice patterns and where there might be connections and disconnections in the system; where there might be stress; or how different people are and where they sit in relation to each other. In addition, you can see where the 'pull' in the system is for each team member/part. In this process, the team maps out each part of the system as they see it, by size, position, orientation, direction. Once all parts are mapped, one can see the relationships between the parts, where the blocks and opportunities might be.

Example 1, mapping the system: A change team composed of external consultants and staff in an energy business were charged with implementing a quality process across a complex and high-risk business. Consultants and staff had contrasting experiences of the team and where their allegiances lay. The consultants experienced tensions between their head office, the department in which they worked and the change team for whom they were advisors and team members. One team member did not depict the team in his drawing at all. This allowed a tough and productive conversation between the leader and the consultant group within the team as to expectations and requirements.

Example 2, mapping the system: An organization was embarking on a cultural change involving a shift in the way decisions were made. We ran the 'organization in the mind' exercise, asking leaders in various teams and groups about the elements and driving factors in decision-making. We noticed that the newer you were, the less the original Charter of the organization was present and therefore the less the original purpose figured in decision-making. This could not have been determined without performing this exercise. It enabled a high pitch of awareness in the senior leader that she needed to ensure that the purpose was re-enforced as a decision-making 'GPS'. This was key for such a purpose-driven organization.

Systems are not complicated, just complex

Complexity theory when applied to organizational human systems, reinforces the fact that though human systems are complex, they are not complicated. Complex human systems act in the way we have been describing because, as in a team, there is connectivity and interdependence between the parts. One action does not just cause a reaction in another part of the system, it causes an action that is 'adaptive', and the ripples of the change continue through the system – some predictable and planned, some not anticipated and unintended. Should the parts of the system become aware of each other's positions, and engage with each other, it is easier for the system to change together, to move together, to perform together (Mitleton-Kelly 2003).

When we can accept that systems are just complex, we can gain a greater understanding of what will influence their complexity. And in doing so, we cannot underestimate the power of assumptions and beliefs in influencing a system and its complexity. When working with an organization, I will always explore with them what they think are the assumptions that are being held in the system, of one part to another and of the system as a whole. We find that people don't notice that they are working in multiple systems at the same time – for instance, a functional team and the senior leadership team. These two roles have different purposes. And as a leader I can move between those different systems, but I do need to be absolutely crystal clear on the purpose of the systems I am working in.

The Adaptable Team Framework is powerful because it gets teams to think about the purpose to which the team is working. First, I need to be aware that I'm working in a number of different systems; second, I need to be aware of the purpose of each of those systems as well as the assumptions governing the way in which systems members take up their roles; third, I might need to challenge or to affirm those assumptions.

What often happens is that leaders don't think this. But it is absolutely essential and if that distinction is not made, it can hold a team back in its sense of itself, its decision-making and its commitment to outcomes. An example may be resource allocation – if senior leadership team members are placing themselves in their functional role, there may well be conflict in the tussle for resources. If those same leaders see their role as serving the organizational system in that moment, they will have a more productive conversation and the organization will be better served.

How would you describe parallel process?

'Parallel process' is a critical and practical concept when working with systems in a team. Smith et al. (1989, 13) described parallel processes as follows: 'when two or more systems – whether these consist of individuals, groups, or organizations – have significant relationships with one another, they tend to develop similar affects, cognition, and behaviours'. This is significant because if a change team starts to mirror the resistance experienced in the rest of the organization, they will struggle to succeed; and if a leadership team mirrors the lack of collaboration in the rest of the organization, it, too, will find instigating better collaboration harder work. Being aware of parallel process is therefore helpful in assisting the team to choose to respond to other parts of the system in a more productive way.

Vignette: A recent example of this from our client work was when, in preparing for a team coaching session for a particular leadership team, we reflected on the fact that we were constantly seeking to finish our tasks and therefore not leaving time to focus on the dynamic of the client team, which was, for us, where the opportunities for that client team lay. Our theory was the client team were avoiding work on the dynamic, feeling that work on the 'task' was 'safer'. We had inadvertently mirrored the client team and we were both therefore avoiding sticky dilemmas within the team dynamics. One system paralleled another.

Systems in a VUCA world

What is a VUCA environment?

The world is going through a highly changeable time. The speed with which old assumptions and rules are being challenged is breath-taking and is fuelled, of course, by the relatively costless and extremely fast exchange of information. For teams in organizations, this means that they need to be highly aware of their environment, and the systems they serve and are influenced by, in order that they can adapt ever more swiftly to both survive and thrive.

Some will be familiar with the term VUCA – a pneumonic standing for volatility, uncertainty, complexity and ambiguity. It was originally devised not by academics but by military strategists and attributed to a General Thurman, of the US Army (Thurman 1991) to aid the development of leadership capabilities of military commanders operating in hostile environments.

The reason that the military believed it was important to describe and categorize such an environment was because VUCA inevitably creates a series of consequences and behavioural traps that leaders and their teams can fall into – and they needed to support leaders to both acknowledge this and respond effectively. The consequences of not being able to do so on a battlefield are obvious. Yet they can be profound for many other sectors away from the military – oil and gas, nuclear fuel, aerospace and transportation, and even in one where there is apparent stability, things can change very quickly.

In a VUCA universe there are high levels of:

- **Volatility:** Things are moving and changing very fast, all the time. It can be highly disorientating and can create both confusion and bewilderment.
- **Uncertainty:** You don't always know what is really happening or when it's going to end, which can create a rising tide of fear and self-doubt that inhibits our ability to focus.
- **Complexity:** An exponential increase in the amount of data that needs to be considered and processed. The normal ways of operating are no longer relevant and often don't work, which can create hesitancy and a reluctance to make any decision in case we get it wrong.
- **Ambiguity:** It is hard to grasp what is really happening, creating a fog where it feels impossible to clarify a clear direction or make decisions.

In the epic poem the *Four Quartets*, T.S. Eliot gives voice to a small bird in the garden: 'humankind cannot bear very much reality'. This plays out in moments of crisis – we shut down. In the classic change cycle (Kubler-Ross 2014), the first stage is denial. This can be translated as a lack of acknowledgement that things have fundamentally changed and that the old rules don't apply. As the Prussian General Moltke once observed, 'no plan survives contact with the enemy'. You have to adapt – and in moving forward – consciously extract learning that supports you and your team to become even more adaptive and resilient. Remarkable things happen when you do.

Chris' story: As a soldier in the 1990s, when my operational experience was far less than many of my colleagues have seen over the last 20 years, I was leading a platoon in Northern Ireland.

A profound lesson for me was that for all the many months of training and preparation for an operational environment, however well we understood what our jobs entailed, and we knew that it was dangerous and that our lives were at risk, it was not until the first 'contact', the first time that somebody tried blow us up, that true reality struck home. The impact of that experience was wide-ranging, but one of the immediate results was a fundamental shift in the attitude and approach of those I was working with. They got that this was now real. I no longer had to check that the simple things were done. There was a new sense of focus and a clear understanding of what was required of each of us, individually and collectively, if we were to do our job well and support each other to survive.

The impact of VUCA on the systems lens

When I was at school and still managing to just about keep up with the physics teaching, I remember a conversation about the application of heat to a substance. If you heat, say, a kettle, the molecules and atoms move faster against each other – and eventually you can see this as a disturbance in the water as it comes to the boil. I still remember this as a useful metaphor for how accelerated change can impact upon a system – even if I stop short of understanding how the science works! We need to be able to retain perspective when things change rapidly, take stock and create a short-term plan to get to the next decision point.

Vignette: One of our clients in the care sector described the rapid narrowing of focus when the pandemic hit, and lockdown was announced. They confirmed three simple goals: 'to keep those we support alive; to keep our colleagues safe and healthy and focused on our first priority; and to develop a fit for purpose organization at the other end of the crisis'. They created what the CEO described as a 'battle rhythm' where an increased regularity of meetings was fed with critical data from which they made both financial and operational decisions. This served them well for the first few weeks by which time a shift of gear was required and also possible as the senior team had stabilized the situation. They then evolved a phased plan comprising 'Recognition and Recuperation', Reconciliation (where colleagues could share feedback), Reflection (on learning), Restitution (getting back to some kind of new normal), Reform (for our new environment) and Reset (the goals and infrastructure to enable the new plans to succeed). Their ability to see the parts of the system and how they related to each other, and the impact of different phases of their response, was impressive and has served them well.

Systems exercise

Bringing the system to life

It is very helpful for a team to experience a system of which they are a part in as live and as real a way as possible. Given the alacrity with which we take up appointed roles, it is not too much of a stretch to ask team members to imagine what it's like to stand in the shoes of other parties within the system they are learning about. The primary purpose of this exercise is to bring the system to life in order that the team can learn more about the different elements might be thinking and feeling. The team can then decide how to create change.

Process

1 Identify a situation that is current for the group – a challenge or problem.
2 Have the group articulate the problem – without reference to cause or assumption of blame.
3 Identify key parties (individuals / groups / stakeholders) and invite volunteers to play each party.
4 What inputs and outputs flow through the system?
5 Invite group members to arrange themselves in the room, in accordance with the way in which they believe the parties are, in the 'system', perhaps under instruction from one or two team members.
6 Pose questions as below with the aim of generating awareness of current state and options for change.

Questions for each party

• What is it like being there for you?
• How do you view each of the other parties / groupings?
• How do you describe your relationship with them?
• What do you need from the other?
• What assumptions are inherent in your position?
• What might you need to do differently?

And . . .

• What needs to change?
• Where does responsibility and accountability lie?
• What is the greatest point of leverage?
• Who is best placed to create a shift?
• How can they be supported?

- What can you do?
- What can the team do?

Example: We worked with the leadership team of a consultancy business, seeking to engage effectively with numerous stakeholders, one of whom was the principal client. There was a complex governance structure in place. We introduced the idea of systems to them and asked them to bring the system to life by placing various team members according to how they experience the system. Not only were team members spread over quite some distance within the room, many of the different elements of the system were engaging with each other at the expense of the customer who felt distinctly left out and in a far corner. By engaging each party and inviting them to articulate the system from their own position, the team was able to see very clearly what they were missing and what they needed to change both within the team as well as across the system.

Summary

- Taking a systems approach is about looking at all parts of a complex human social system and how those parts relate to each other.
- By leaders embracing a systems approach it is easier to initiate and lead change and place resources and influence where they are most needed.
- There are various ways to bring a system to life for a team, such that team members can both make sense of what is happening, clarify their part in that system and make decisions about what they will do.
- In a VUCA environment – one that is volatile, uncertain, complex and ambiguous – the need to take a systems view is even more important and can help a team anticipate and lead change and adapt well.

Team purpose

Who we are, is all we have

Who we are in a team and who the team members want to be together is instrumental. It is the driving force behind the team's ability to serve the system and to lead and deliver effectively for stakeholders. The more the team is clear about its own identity as a team and what its purpose is, the more commitment it will bring to its work and the more effective it will be as a team.

This chapter examines the importance of a team defining its purpose and the opportunity that affords for greater unity and cohesion as well as a robust identity and sense of itself. All of these are critical for the team to be able to lead others together and influence change in the wider organization. A central part of this chapter is the way in which that purpose and therefore the team's role can be arrived at. We use the Transforming Experience Framework (TEF) to achieve this.

Purpose I

'A Blueprint for a Better Business' expresses the 'purpose of purpose' for an organization as an opportunity to inspire and reveal the human face of the organization, connect what it says with what it does, and reinforce its interdependence with the world around it. Businesses that have a robust purpose that fulfils these criteria have more engaged employees who are more innovative, more loyal customers and suppliers, receptive communities and regulators, and the organization becomes an attractive prospect to future employees.

We would argue that the same intention and outcomes are appropriate for a team. If one does encapsulate the purpose of the team beyond the delivery of business goals, it becomes the lodestar for the team and a core touch point when making decisions in the team. One might say that if one is in a leadership team the purpose of the team is therefore to lead. But what does this mean? In what way will the team lead? Who will it be serving if it is leading? By leading, what is it seeking to generate for the organization beyond specific metrics and outputs? What kind of organization does it wish to create in its leadership? How authentic is the team being in expressing how it wants to lead what it wishes its contribution to be?

One of my favourite scenes among many, from *Butch Cassidy and the Sundance Kid*, is when our two heroes are being pursued into the hills overlooking the Mojave Desert. Every time they look back, they see the posse coming after them led by a mysterious tracker in a straw hat. And every time they look back they look at each other and ask, 'who are those guys?' In a sense, that's what your staff are doing when they look at the leadership team. They're asking, 'who are those guys, what do they represent, what's important to them, what do they value, what will they do for me?'

The unique purpose of the team will be crafted from the clarity that the team has in what is required by stakeholders, as well as the impact that the team truly wishes to make on the stakeholders and the difference it wants to make to their work, perhaps even to their broader lives. So, the team's purpose is a woven article, not a single strand. It is not a political manifesto that simply seeks to gain power by gathering votes, it is something deeply felt and meaningful to the team. It springs from the heart as well as the head. It is similar to the idea that each senior person will dispatch their role in different ways – despite the fact that their objectives may be the same from one person to the next. They will see their role differently, they will have a different sense of themselves, which they translate into different priorities and they may bring their unique authority that is personal to them. It is the same for a team – the team brings its unique identity into play as a result of the way it sees its purpose. So, having a team purpose and declaring it, is a leadership act.

Opening discussions on why the team exists and then arriving at a clear statement to encapsulate that purpose, also initiates the building, through alignment, of two team qualities that make it easier for the team to deliver – unity and cohesion.

- **Unity:** Unity in a team is very helpful. It is helpful because when working on decisions that are about team outcomes, and that team is a leadership team, it will need to communicate those decisions clearly and meaningfully to those the team leads. Without a sense of unity within the team, that will not occur. Messages will be confused, they will be given and received differently, and the result will be confusion away from the team. So, having practical unity is important. Unity is important for another reason too, and that is because without unity, trust within the team is eroded – because team members may start to believe others cannot be relied upon; and between the team and the outside world because the team is not experienced by others as speaking with one voice and can be 'played' off against each other. Many times, we have seen the relationship between contractor teams and client teams become strained, with seemingly few avenues for real collaboration despite both teams talking a good collaborative game. That sense of 'one' endeavour is seen to be untrue. And as soon as that happens, then most of the best conversations happen away from the joint endeavour and the team is weakened.

- **Cohesion:** Cohesion describes 'the degree to which team members desire to remain in the team and are committed to the goal' (Forsyth 2009). 'High cohesive groups are more effective than low cohesive groups in achieving their respective goals' (Shaw 2011). The more cohesive the team, all other things being equal, the better.

Questions for team purpose

There are two principal ways of supporting a team to generate its purpose. The simplest is to pose a series of questions to the team:

- What do I believe is the reason this team exists?
- Who are the primary stakeholders of this team and what do they need from us?
- When this team does its job well, what difference does it make to its customers, to its people and to the organization?

Once discussion has been had and consensus reached, a form of words is arrived at that may be finessed over time but requires support from the whole team. Team members may not share this purpose with others, though often choose to do so – if they do, it increases the accountability they experience for delivering on the team's purpose.

The second method is a 'deeper dive' and for us yields a more powerful expression of the team's real contribution as a team to the systems that they serve. We cover this approach, the 'TEF', in the next section.

Here are three examples of leadership team purposes and what they enable the teams to do and achieve:

Leadership team of Leading Alliances Inc.

After conversations about stakeholders and their needs, their current performance position, how everyone thought and felt about being in role and the opportunities that the team had, they posed the question to themselves: What is this team striving to achieve by X?

Here is what they came up with: 'One team delivering outcomes to maximize return for the business.'

Underneath this they listed items like 'seen as partner', 'deliver to time, cost and quality' and 'zero harm'. This, for them, was an expression of who they were and why they were together.

This team used this purpose and the goals that sat underneath it as their continual point of reference. They created an accessible version of purpose, vision and goals, which they and, over time, their colleagues referred to in order to make decisions and track progress. The team was marked by key stakeholders as one of the most successful teams in the business.

Operations leadership team within Major Energy plc

- We serve staff and the Major Energy plc executive.
- To lead our operation to generate success: financial performance, engagement, external customers.
- To ensure we run an effective and efficient business.
- To be clear on our vision for the future and our performance expectations.

- To transform the business.
- To enact Major Energy plc purpose, values, ambitions and leadership approach.

They also created a 'declaration', a picture of success that as a team they were aiming for:

We are ONE TEAM, mutually accountable for:

- The generation of enduring achievements, which are recognized outside of our department. We are committed to delivering to our business colleagues, a measured and accurate service.
- We visibly display alignment through an integrated and synchronized approach by pulling in the same direction. We understand each other's goals, roles and responsibilities, and value our diverse business knowledge.
- Our leadership is innovative, pro-active and resilient. We focus on a virtuous cycle of continuous improvement. We take time to celebrate.
- We are disciplined, ambitious, have an effective governance process and we care for each other.

As a result of working on their purpose in this way and using it as a touch point for progress and their sense of unity as a team, they were able to lead a major restructuring and outsourcing process, substantially reducing cost and improving service delivery.

Leadership team of Large Innovation Projects plc

Here is an example of a team that was overseeing projects worth c. £1.5 bn.

'To lead our united organization to deliver new and imaginative projects through releasing and inspiring our people to innovate, excel and create a legacy of which we can all be proud.'

From a challenging start, the team was able to deliver the business value required of them and created a clear and combined identity for their organization, which to that point had been missing, and a team spirit that they had, to that point, struggled to initiate.

Purpose II

The Transforming Experience Framework: connecting purpose with role and action

This is a lens through which we can look at a number of different areas relating to team functioning, but ones that operate at a deeper level of learning because they are about the team's sense of itself. For the team it is saying 'this is who we are and how we express the best of ourselves through our roles as a team'.

Background

My colleague Elana Friedman was working in the early 2000s with John Bazalgette from the Grubb Institute, a faith-based organization that carries out organizational development globally and has done since the 1990s. John and Elana were working in educational institutions. The Institute's approach is research and evidenced-based and it has its roots in psychoanalysis. The full title of the model is 'Transforming Experience into Authentic Action through Role' (Long 2016), which is material to its use in organizations – each word in the title would have resonance for many readers – in particular, it draws attention to authentic action, authentic role.

It is a useful model in that it draws together in one place a very clear articulation of how individual leaders 'take up' their role and lead and how a team can do the same.

Notes on leadership

For us, leadership is not something you get because you have a title, it's a role that you choose to 'take up'. In any organization, we have lots of leaders who aren't choosing to take the role of leadership because they don't see themselves as such and because they're not formally leaders. Conversely, lots do take up leadership despite not having a title.

The TEF helps teams and individual leaders (regardless of where they are in the system) be clear on how they can take up the role of leadership in the most effective manner. It also addresses three levels that are key in taking up leadership – self leadership, team leadership and system leadership, and do so 'at scale' so that different parts of the system can be connected more effectively.

One of the things that traditional leadership development can miss is helping leaders be clear on how they can contribute at those different levels in a nimble and adaptable way. By using this approach with teams, significant clarity can be brought to what the team is for and how leaders can make their greatest contribution.

The framework

Figure 7.1 The Transforming Experience Framework
Connecting Purpose with Role and Action (Long 2016)

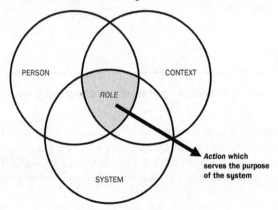

The framework consists of three circles:

1 **The personal, the self:** Each of us brings ourselves into any particular role. That can be unconsciously or consciously. The more we can consciously bring ourselves into role, the more powerful we can be in our leadership of others. That shift involves knowing and identifying our assumptions, being able to challenge them, and knowing and identifying our preferences, desires and triggers. It's about knowing the effect we are likely to have on the context within which we work.

2 **The system:** We are all in one system or another and all of us are also in multiple systems. Often, we invite team members to map the multiple systems in their lives – their community, faith, family, business and, of course, the teams at work, which are themselves systems. Some are informal – the running group, the smoking group (remember those?), which used to be a very powerful system because it was one of the few that was cross departmental but had a shared purpose. We all sit in multiple systems. You have to know which system you are in at any given point – and remember that each system has a different purpose. The team also sits in and potentially serves different systems – consider the Health, Safety and the Environment team, for instance. It will serve all of the operational leadership 'systems', for example, the executive team, and the staff group, as a whole system. The starting point here is being clear on which system one is in at any given moment.

3 **The context:** Once you have become aware of the systems you are in and perhaps selected one to focus on, you then examine the context within which that system sits – and so consider the rest of the organization, the sector, the government, regulators, many of which are stakeholders. If you are a senior leader, it's not about ignoring your global role for instance, or your company purpose, it's just taking the systems lens and seeing the context within which your chosen system sits. So, the context is the wider system but not the primary one on which you are focusing your attention.

In using this approach, the boundary of the system that you focused on becomes clear – who is in and who is out. The next thing is about understanding the purpose of that system – it'll be different to the other systems that you are party to. For instance, we can make the distinction between a functional leadership role and a global role that oversees the whole enterprise.

Example: You are a product development lead, bringing all your professional experience and standards and expectations to the team; your system is the product development function, the products team, where the purpose is to create the most innovative product to support the business; in the context there are things that will influence you – health and safety regulations, a 3 per cent cut in budget, the attitude of the sales function, and, of course, ultimately customers. All of those things can influence the way you take up your role, but primarily you take a role in service of the system purpose, so ensure that you know what system you are in and you know what the system purpose is, too.

Your role comes last, it's about taking up your role in an organization and in a team in a way that is purposeful and clear and that is connected to the purpose that the system is trying to achieve. There can sometimes be lots of activity without a lot of results and that is often because of a lack of clarity of purpose. People are doing lots of stuff and are very busy, but it's not purposeful action.

In short, the TEF encourages you to continuously be checking:

- What system am I in?
- What's the purpose of the system?
- How do I take up my role as a leader or a team member in a way that most serves the purpose of the system?

This is a really helpful tool on multiple levels, from the day-to-day to the long term.

At the day-to-day level, I may be going to a meeting and I can consider these three questions above. You might also ask:

- What do I need to notice about myself?
- What assumptions am I holding?
- What are my hopes and anxieties?

All these things influence the way in which I take up my role as a leader or as a team member. It can literally be a moment to prepare before you go into a meeting, so that you can most effectively take up your role in that meeting.

All the teams we work with have this problem – individuals might be over-identifying with one leadership role – for instance, their functional leadership role, which is less helpful when they are in an executive team charged with leading the enterprise as a whole. It enables you to be 'system savvy' because at any given moment you become clearer about the multiple systems at play and those things that will pull you in different directions. This helps you to stay on track.

Vignette: A senior leader in the global leadership team asks, 'How do I take up my role?' Five minutes earlier she was in a GLT meeting where she was expected to take up her role as a GLT member and her function would be in the 'context'. Now she is in a functional meeting, wearing a different hat, serving another system in the organization. She does not let go of that previous role, because the GLT role and that other system will still influence her. She needs to remain clear: What is the purpose I am working to and therefore how will I take up my role?

Leaders may consider their roles to be an 'either-or' choice – either GLT or functional lead in the previous example. This is a false choice – it is 'both-and', though the emphasis will change depending on the system you are focusing on. It is therefore a change in mindset.

Where the three areas meet: powerful leadership

You are most 'powerfully' in role, not when you are purely sitting in your chosen system space. You are most powerfully in role in the centre, where the three areas meet. You are equally acknowledging and drawing on yourself, on your own purpose, and what you stand for; on what's going on in the context; and what's going on in the system. But all the while, you are working to the system purpose – in our case, to the team purpose.

It connects well with the Adaptable Team Framework: the key driver is not just what system you are in but what is the purpose of that system.

Vignette: Consider that meeting you were recently in. Think about what role you took up in the meeting. What purpose do you think you were working to – were you clear on which purpose you were working to? It may become clear why the team didn't get the result it was looking for and why the conversation was so difficult – because actually there were four of you in that conversation and what the team didn't appreciate is that we were now in the R&D system rather than in 'product design', or engineering, and therefore you were all pulling in opposite directions. You didn't stop and go, 'okay, so what's the purpose? Now, how do we support one another within the purpose of the R&D system?' which is different to the product design and engineering system. How could that meeting have been improved, using the TEF lens?

We will often get team members to think about whether they know the purpose of every system they are in and whether they can define it. Often, a lot of teams are actually unclear about what their purpose is – so if we can help a team to be clear, it is significantly more likely to encourage team members to align and bring themselves fully to the team at each interaction.

Team purpose to individual role

Once the purpose of the team is clear, each team member can ask themselves and each other: 'What do I need to turn the volume up on, what do I need to turn the volume down on, in order to be able to be most in role in service to that purpose? Who else might I need to enrol? What other conversations do I think I need to be having? What happens when I get pulled into the 'personal' part of the model? What happens if I forget which system I am in? What conversations do I need to have to keep myself in that sweet spot?'

A word on purpose and delivery goals

The purpose of any team is greater than their task. For instance, the marketing team's purpose can be 'marketing the organization's services'. It also might be to create content that enables the organization to attract great clients or great talent, or its purpose could be that they support the public to see their organization as one where staff and customers feel at home. The purpose is the team's GPS.

Leadership team of major continuous improvement

From the TEF conversations with a change leadership team, they created the following purpose, supporting them to progress their project with the support of the executive team.

(Given that) 'Lean Is the Way We Work' the team's purpose is to be:

- Enablers and catalysts towards a shift of a continuous improvement mindset by operationalizing Lean.

And to:

- Translate Lean into day-to-day business.
- Challenge the business to identify and 'size' performance improvement opportunities and hold it to account for following through on improvement plans.
- Support the creation and implementation of a CI process and rhythm.

Identity

Purpose and identity

Having open conversations about why the team exists and its purpose is, of course, a process of alignment and agreement. It allows individuals to express what they wish to see happen and what is important to them in being part of the team. Being able to respond to a question 'why do we exist?' has an intimate relationship with the team members' social identity.

Personal identity is about how we conceive of ourselves both at a conscious as well as subconscious level – our traits, preferences, motivations, values and beliefs, and in addition, over time, how our experiences have shaped us and the choices that we have made. Our social identity, however, is how we conceive of ourselves in relation to others and specifically the groups of which we choose to be a part. If we have a hand in forming what it means to be in a particular team, then we have a chance to create an additional element of our social identity as an individual as well as contribute to the identity of the team – how the team conceives of itself.

Clearly how we conceive of ourselves when we engage with others has an impact on how we think and feel about ourselves and others and the behaviour we exhibit towards them. Exactly the same is true of teams and the building of a team identity.

There is a philosophical element to this that is translated into the fabric of psychology through how it is that we create our social identity. That is, that given that we are highly social creatures wired to seek out others with whom we can collaborate – to achieve both material and emotional gain – it is again difficult to think of our identity actually being separate at all from others.

I am lucky to have built strong friendships with some senior client leaders; one such is Roger Laing, VP of RLG International, a rather special global consultancy. He won't mind me saying that one of his favourite aphorisms, in part personally crafted, is 'you are how you show up'. He leads an organization where early on in our relationship one of his team stopped us in a workshop that we were conducting to say, 'David, no, you don't understand. When we arrive on an oil rig to support the OIM and their team, the OIM usually asks our team "who are you, what do you want, and when are you leaving?"' It is at that very moment that the arriving consultancy team needs to show up not just well and looking like they know what they are doing, but with a very clear sense of purpose and feeling themselves, inside, as though they are meant to be there. Although 'faking it while you make it' can go some way to bridging the gap – and indeed is an identifiable therapeutic process in some circumstances, for a team that is seeking to influence those they lead, other teams in the business, clients, and the broader stakeholder system, being truly authentic, and providing leadership that is felt by the team to be true to who they are and what they wish to achieve, is crucial.

Identity – how we create our social identity

There are three steps by which we as individuals form our social identity (Turner, Brown and Tajfel 1979):

- The first is to categorize oneself and others. This saves time and ensures that we know how to behave with different groups of people. Accuracy is sacrificed (we may respond to individuals differently) but it means we can predict what might happen depending on where we are and who we are with.
- Next, we identify ourselves with a particular group. We are members of lots of groups in society – families, schools, colleges, organizations, sports teams. We identify probably more with one group than another, though this changes over time.
- The third ingredient to our social identity is comparison of our group with others. It develops our self-esteem and self-confidence to believe that our group is in some way superior to others.

Message for teams: build your identity so others know who you are . . .

Early on in the life of the team, its identity is fragile. It is a collection of individuals who are being nice to each other and making a valiant attempt to be clear on the task in hand. It builds rules, as we've discussed, to make it feel like it's making some decisions that will help regulate the quality of the relationships and the conversations that it has together. And it may even define how it wishes to function more broadly and the kind of team it wishes to be, again, as we discussed. And yet there's no getting away from the fact that helping the team see that it is different and distinct from other teams, and perhaps even better than other teams, can help bolster its sense of self. This is a natural process.

. . . and remain open to the influence of those outside the team

Yet that very process can make the team less permeable, less open to influence. In any relationship if there is an imbalance or inequity, a sense of unfairness will emerge. With teams, as with individuals. So, while reinforcing the sense of discrete separateness and distinction from others – even uniqueness in its role and purpose, the team needs to be careful that it stays open to being influenced by others, which requires good listening of each other and therefore of other teams and other parties in the system. A team whose identity is so separate and so strong will become remote, and unable to influence, unable to lead.

Our experience is that actively building identity through discussions and declaration of team purpose is a crucial ingredient in alignment. Without team members being aligned with each other, it will be difficult for the team to make good decisions together and engage in co-ordinated action to get results. Once the team has gained in confidence and gained a more stable and aligned identity and is clear on its true purpose, role and sense of self, it is confident enough to challenge the status quo, to really lead change and to know when it is doing that such that they 'have each other's backs'.

Vignette on identity: We worked with a utility senior leadership team bringing together 10 people from seven different organizations. The entity had a name, and a brand, but no single bank account, and systems and processes that didn't seem to fit together. Those individual leaders, though very capable, struggled in the early days to work effectively together, in part because there remained a strong emotional pull to their 'home' organization. The team focused a lot early in its life together on its sense of identity, building its clear purpose – and lots of small things like having a common email postfix, and as has been suggested early on, solving problems together, and getting to know and understand where everybody was 'coming from'. Bit by bit, they were able to assemble a very powerful team. The team exceeded expectations on delivery. This was due, in no small part, to the effort that each team member and notably the leader put into creating a sense of unified purpose and identity for the team, both inside the team as well as with the rest of the business they led.

Summary

- Early on in the life of the team, it is important to agree why it exists – to articulate the purpose of the team. This goes beyond simple delivery of goals and expresses the difference the team will make to stakeholders and perhaps to the world beyond.
- This process of aligning behind a common purpose enables the team to build unity, which aids the building of trust; as well as the development of cohesion in the team, both of which have a material impact on the team's ability to deliver results.

- A straightforward and a more in-depth process for the team to articulate its purpose is available.
- The Transforming Experience Framework enables the team to connect the purpose of the team to its practical role and contribution, and to the actions that it will take.
- The articulation of purpose, role and action of the team allows it to build its identity, which supports the development of individual and collective confidence and therefore its ability to deliver.

8 | Team results

Results are not what they were

When you embark upon a performance journey, aiming to deliver a result – an outcome or output – you also create other outcomes and outputs along the way. These additional outcomes and outputs are sowing the seeds for future excellence or future failure. Knowing what they are, therefore, and being able to assess them as you go becomes important. As Churchill may well not have said: 'However beautiful the strategy, you should occasionally look at the results'. Without paying attention to them, the team will not thrive.

In this chapter we expand the meaning of results and look at exactly what is produced when a team engages in a performance journey. We look at the fact that many organizations now don't just assess 'performance' but how that performance is produced. It is important to assess a team's output, as well as levels of enjoyment, learning and meaning, all as results that the team generates as it works together.

What is team effectiveness?

Being efficient is about economy of effort, minimizing waste; being effective is about getting a result. Yet if you are going to measure effectiveness for a team, what results are you interested in? What confuses matters a little is that what you produce as a result of your effort is not just the outcome you wanted but other outputs that make your future results more or less possible.

Once again, I reach for Hackman (1990, 272) to assist in confirming what are the most significant outputs and outcomes that are relevant to team effectiveness: 'the productive output of the team (as assessed by clients of the team); the enhanced capability of the team to perform interdependently in the future; the individual learning, growth, and personal well-being of individual team members'.

Team results are not just about performance

A little while ago, I worked with a senior leadership team in a FTSE 100 company, which was grappling with how to measure its 'performance'. Team members received a bonus on delivering against particular key performance indicators (KPIs), and both individual and team outcomes would be under the microscope, which created an edge to the conversation, as you can imagine.

One section of the KPIs, recently introduced into that business, was not on *what* was to be delivered, the output, but on *how* it was delivered. This was a new indicator of 'performance'. It was about values, behaviours, relationships and leadership qualities displayed, and how staff felt about the leadership team. It seems that one of the great pop tie-ups of the 1980s, The Fun Boy Three and Bananarama, were close to the truth in declaring: 'It's not what you do, it's the way that you do it, and that's what gets results'.

Why is 'how you do it' so important for a 'result'? Studies show that satisfaction is both an outcome and antecedent of success in a task. How satisfied people are is material to the performance you are seeking to create and its sustainability over time. Increasingly, organizations are interested not just in the outputs but in the manner in which you achieved them. If you achieved them leading the team being an unpleasant and feared leader, and your team then left the business, that impairs the ability of the organization to get results in the future. So, both are important. In addition, for me, it's important because in an age in which short-term and easy gain has arguably caused so much damage to the world economy, we need to look at how to create performance that is sustainable – and that requires us to look at other measures of outcome rather than just output. Let's look at this from the leadership team's perspective.

No good hitting the numbers this year and then witnessing an exodus of team members because they can't stand being in the business a moment longer. If they deliver but feel burnt out, unwell, unappreciated and as if they are stagnating, that won't help the business. And customers get this too – they know what quality looks like. If the product is great but the customer service is shocking (because you are not leading it well because, let's face it, all things are connected), they will not buy.

Team results are not only down to performance, but also learning, enjoyment and meaning. For some time now, we have been inviting teams and individual leaders we work with to look at what they wish to create and what they are already creating though may not be aware of. We ask them to rate each of the following four areas in relation to their work together, out of 10 – both on how it is now as well as how they would like it to be:

1 **Performance:** How is the team performing? What output is being created? To what degree is the team delivering to the standard expected from stakeholders? Is it delivering to time, to cost, to the quality that is required? What is its health and safety record?

2 **Learning:** Are team members learning together, expanding their collective capacity to deliver? Are they developing the knowledge skills and abilities that will assist team delivery and longer-term careers? Are they repeating success in a previous role or are their skills and experience being utilized and stretched to their satisfaction?

3 **Enjoyment:** Is the team a source of joy and satisfaction, adding a spring to their step? Do they look forward to pursuing the team's goals? If they are a member of a number of teams, to what extent would they regard this team

as their home team, the one to which they truly belong and therefore will contribute discretionary effort? Are team members physically and emotionally well, free of undue stress and insoluble wicked problems?

4 **Meaning:** Is the team pursuing something important, something that is meaningful to team members? Something they can share with others and be proud of being part of? Having a meaningful endeavour that contributes to a wider cohort – perhaps for some having an importance to society, to the local area, to staff – is important for team members' mental health and is increasingly material to the decisions of millennials coming into the workforce, for whom the values of the organization they join and the degree to which they are in evidence is the difference between staying or going.

The proposition, therefore, is that each of these areas contributes to a sustainable result. The more team members can learn together, the more powerful they will be together; the more they enjoy their work as a team, the more they will produce; the more meaningful they find their work, the more they will put in that discretionary effort, go the extra mile.

On meaning and enjoyment

Human beings are meaning-making machines. We make the behaviours of others, events, coincidences, objects, houses, chapters in our lives, mean something. So it is with teams and their team members. What does being a member of this team mean to me? What is our purpose and is it worthwhile? Will this get me out of bed in the morning knowing we are doing important work? And, importantly, even if it is important work, will my wish to deliver be blunted by the experience? Will I find the work so enjoyable I wish to recommit for the next round, another year?

If we buy that some of the outputs to teamwork can help the team create sustainable results, then it is worth looking at those outputs too.

Both meaning and enjoyment are positive emotions one can derive from engaging with a task. It is worth drawing on the work of Martin Seligman and his leadership of positive psychology at this point. His work as a clinical psychologist, subsequent leadership of the American Psychological Society (APS), and creation of the first MSc in Positive Psychology at Pennsylvania State University has made him a household name in psychology circles. Positive psychology is not the same as positive thinking. Positive thinking stands a good chance of helping one live in a fantasy world, where you ignore events material to you and believe that you can jump off tall buildings and fly. Positive psychology, on the other hand, is 'the scientific study of what makes life most worth living' (Peterson, Park and Sweeney 2008, 20). I would argue that if your team does not contribute to a life worth living, then you need to find a different team, or help lead the team in a different direction. Seligman's own work makes an important distinction between different levels of experience and how they can be achieved. He uses the term 'signature strengths' to represent aspects of our character that give us strength. They may not be things that we are immediately good at but that make us strong and help us make our best contribution.

- **The Pleasant Life:** Pursues positive emotion about the past, present and the future.
- **The Good life:** Uses signature strengths, which leads to greater sense of gratification.
- **The Meaningful Life:** Uses signature strengths in service of something larger than the self.

Meaning is taken to represent, at a simple level, feeling that what you do is 'valuable and worthwhile' (Seligman 2011) and that it contributes to something in the world beyond you. In refining his approach, Seligman created his well-being assessment under the following headings: Positive emotions, Engagement, Relationships, Meaning and Accomplishment (PERMA), an assessment that we have used in tracking progress in executive coaching engagements. In a world where a lack of good mental health is becoming an increasing concern and recognized as material to the health and therefore performance of organizations, it is useful to assess meaning and enjoyment as part of the journey towards sustainable performance and teams that can adapt to their environment.

On learning

We shall look more at the importance of learning as part of the generation of sustainable results in a later chapter. It is important to note here that learning is not just important to be able to support the team to be successful. It is critical for good mental health too. Those who continue to learn throughout their lives benefit from a range of health outcomes including protection and recovery from mental illness, and the ability to cope with major illness; in addition, learning raises self-esteem (self-worth) and self-efficacy (confidence) and lends a sense of purpose and aids social integration to one's life (Hammond 2004). When one is highly capable one's role offers opportunity for 'mastery experiences'; it can create a major positive impact, re-enforcing a sense of one's individual and social identity. A recent LinkedIn survey (LinkedIn 2018) reported that 93 per cent of employees would stay at a company if it invested in their careers. The same survey noted that the top four skills that employees needed to acquire were soft skills – communication, leadership, time management and collaboration – all of these require practice in the field, and one could argue can only really be acquired in role. In Deloitte's Global Human Capital Report (2017) provision of growth opportunities was identified as one of the central factors in provision of a good employee experience. So, learning in a modern organization is not just a nice to have, it is core to engagement and has a material impact on the bottom line. In a team, as in the wider organization, our experience is that knowing things is not sufficient, it's about applying that learning in increasingly complex and challenging circumstances and learning as you go.

Collective learning in a team enriches and accelerates the learning experience and gives opportunities for those mastery experiences, which builds capability and raises confidence. Learning is therefore again, not a nice to have, but an essential – for the team to gain sustainable results and for team members to stay, grow and be healthy.

Invite the team to assess itself

The four elements that go to make up the results can be turned into a kite or diamond, with each element rated on a scale of 0–10. To help, we put this in a pictorial form on a flip chart. The scoring can be done at a break in the session, inviting private scoring by turning the flip chart into the corner of the room.

Once done, the team can examine the clustering of their anonymous scores. These questions can contribute to the all-important conversation that can then ensue:

1 Where is the team now and what has contributed to that?
2 Where would the team like to be and what makes this compelling?
3 What can you do, individually and collectively, to move this forward?

Figure 8.1 The Diamond Model

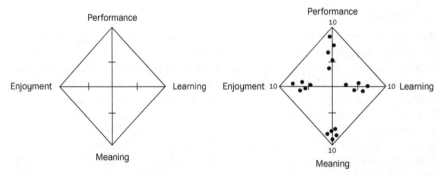

Team members start to share what is important for them, what they need to be successful and how they will reach and sustain performance.

This becomes a 'jumping off point' for a whole raft of conversations from goal setting, to how they lead the business through to the culture they create. The more practical and focused the conversation, the more alignment there will be. The more alignment, the more successful the team will be.

Numerous teams we have worked with find this exercise a great bridge to the wider questions of corporate measurement – realizing that if they can be aware of their own sustainable results as a team, then it is easier to connect that with their ability to lead others.

So that's what gets *sustainable* results . . .

Summary

- Team effectiveness is defined as 'the productive output of the team, the enhanced capability of the team to perform in the future, the individual learning, growth and personal well-being of individual team members' (Hackman and Wageman 2002, 272).
- More organizations are interested not just in performance (output) of the team but how that performance was produced.
- We see it is critical to the team's ability to create sustainable results that it tracks progress on its performance, as well as its learning, the enjoyment of team members and the meaning that team members hold for the work they do together in the team.
- At a simple level, focusing on all four elements will ensure that team members are able to improve each of them more easily.
- Importantly for the organization, it gives the team the opportunity to retain and engage effective leaders and ensure their ongoing health and well-being.

9 Team action

Practise your best shots

Successful coordinated action occurs when the team pays attention to and gets really good at a few fundamental 'teamship' activities. In this chapter, we look at seven fundamentals that team members need to be really good at and ways in which they can keep on practising those best shots. We examine how the team can, with the leader's and the coach's help, get good at:

- Setting direction
- Agreeing roles and developing accountability
- Making sound decisions
- Innovating
- Making good use of difference
- Supporting and challenging.

We look at each of them in turn and see how the coach and leader can support a team in following through on them. As a successful senior client of ours often reminds his team, 'keep on practising your best shots', so practice does indeed make perfect.

Setting direction

Goals and maps

Team goal setting for direction

It is perhaps the most obvious and well-known element of teamwork that having a clear goal set is important. On my bookshelf I still have an original copy of Peter Drucker's *Practice of Management*, published in 1954, and his work continues to reverberate around the corporate world today. *Intentional Behaviour* was published in 1970 (Ryan 1970), containing the theory behind goals. Perhaps the title of the book gives us a very useful lead-in as to why goal setting works and how it is best used with a team.

Locke and Latham picked up the goal-setting banner and worked initially in the logging industry examining the effect of goal setting on a variety of variables including productivity. Researchers and organizations have long known that there is 'a strong evidentiary basis for the performance effect of goals' in teams (Guzzo and Dickson 1996, 337–308). 'In short, goal setting theory is among the most valid and practical theories of employee motivation in organisational psychology' (Locke and Latham 2002).

Why does goal setting work?

Knowing how goal setting works is useful because it allows you to observe the team and see whether helpful responses are being triggered, what might be getting in the way, and whether the goals need to be adjusted. Goals work because they trigger four responses in the team. These are that the team's attention is directed towards goal relevant activities, team members are physically energized, they become more persistent in their activity, and the search for knowledge and new strategies is initiated.

What can the team and the leader do to magnify the motivational effect?

The team can make its goals public, which many teams choose to do to assist with communication with staff (this triggers an external accountability); they can take opportunities to formulate task strategies together; and they can construct an effective and trusted feedback process. Organizations being the complex organisms they are, getting feedback that is fit for your goals and nice and simple can be tricky but worth it. The leader can express genuine confidence in the team's ability to find a way to reach the goals and can set the expectation that the team will devise strategies and solve problems together. In addition, it is motivational if the leader behaves supportively and establishes an inspiring picture or vision of success with which the team members can identify with, personally.

Tips on difficulty, learning goals and alignment

- Set difficult goals. This leads to higher performance and triggers greater interest in the required tasks because 'difficult goals consistently (lead) to higher performance than urging people to do their best' (Locke and Latham 2002, 705–717).
- Set learning goals when the goals are complex. This lowers anxiety and encourages a better search for effective strategies (Winters and Latham 1996).
- Ensure goals are aligned with the team member's goals. An obvious one maybe, but not only is the team's performance enhanced if there is alignment, but without such alignment, 'personal goals have a detrimental effect' (Seijts and Latham 2000).

When setting goals, remember great goals have these characteristics

As a team sets its goals therefore, it is useful to remember that great goals are:

- **Small in number**, so as not to be forgotten easily
- **Challenging,** encouraging confidence

- **Outcomes** (not activities) – not a shopping list of actions
- **Compelling** in that they trigger the creative search for delivery strategies
- **Important** to stakeholders and to the team
- **Aligned** within and outside the team
- **Not conflicting**, avoiding turf wars.

Vignette: With a three-party joint venture leadership team, we spent some time early on supporting them in crafting the appropriate goal set with specific measures. They were keen to be able to share those goals with the organization they led and do it in a memorable way. They enlisted the support of a graphic artist who translated them into engaging pictures without losing the clarity of goal they had generated. It made them easily referred to and communicated to others. It really bought them to life. Given the nature of their work together and the requirements of stakeholders, they did not change for the two and a half years they worked together, surviving changes in leader, team members and stakeholder situation. They contributed to the creation of a high performing team.

Figure 9.1 Bringing Goals Alive

New wave goal setting: OKRs

OKR stands for objectives and key results. This is a modern build on 'management by objectives' and aims to be both clear and simple as well as highly motivational – so it retains psychological properties of goal setting. Taking the original work by Andy Gove who devised the process within Intel, John Doerr (2018) in *Measure What Matters* explains the very simple process now famously used by Google and one that is now embraced by many organizations particularly in the technology sector. Described by Doerr and his colleagues as 'KPIs' with soul, they reflect a flexibility and ambition resonant of the tech sector where being able to 'pivot' quickly is crucial. In fact, KPIs may be seen as 'good key results' that are adjusted to retain focus.

An objective (in the OKR language another word for goal) is the 'what'. Objectives are bold, audacious outcomes, the 'highest priorities you need to accomplish', and are often agreed for the shorter term than many organizations are used to – say 30–90 days. One organization we work with resets them every quarter for the business and the senior team, and each individual follows suit to ensure complete alignment.

A key result is the measurable benchmark that you can use to track progress towards your objective. Key results are the 'how' and taken together lead you to achieve your objective, which in turn contributes to your mission/vision as an organization.

Flexibility is emphasized by Doerr. The OKR cadence his team recommends is 90 days though, even within that period, objectives might show themselves to be less relevant and needing to be adjusted or dropped. And every 90 days therefore there is an opportunity to retain the objectives, adjust the key results, or drop or change out the objectives. For a team this keeps the focus fresh and energizing. Part of the spirit of goal setting therefore becomes a key ingredient in the process. Our client teams who embrace this have found it refreshing and enjoy the flexibility, allowing them to adapt more quickly. Their ability to set good goals is also enhanced so takes less time and the habit of tracking progress is embedded.

An example: Google Chrome team (Doerr 2018)

Objective: 'to build the next generation web browser'

- **Key result (2008):** Reach 20 million daily active users
- **Key result (2009):** Reach 50 million daily active users
- **Key result (2010):** Reach 100 million daily active users.

How do you support a team to set team goals?

A team goal-setting process

Invite the team to engage with the following question (individually and then together).

- What do we need to achieve to fulfil our purpose? (brainstorm)

Once they have flushed out a number of specifics, they can then sift through them. Invite the team to engage with the following questions (individually and then together):

- What do we need to achieve to fulfil our purpose? (brainstorm)
- Once they have flushed out a number of specifics, they can then sift through them:
- If we deliver on these goals to what extent will we deliver on our purpose?
- If we deliver on these goals to what extent will we meet stakeholder need?
- Which simple metrics will we use?

Once you have an emerging goal set, the team can then apply the MECE rule – are the goals in front of you:

- **Mutually exclusive:** Are they distinct and separate from each other, not overlapping and therefore producing potential conflict?
- **Collectively exhaustive:** Taken together they attend to all of what needs to be achieved.

Then, the team can prioritize, nominating a lead executive who will take them forward.

Roadmaps for direction

For every journey you need a map. Our day-to-day experience of maps, however, is now of the digital variety and quite often we don't think about where we are going before we set off, relying almost totally on the satellite navigation system in our phone. Map-reading skills are on the decline – which personally I think is a shame given the amount of understanding and imagination that can be triggered so richly by looking at a map if you have learnt to interpret them, especially if you are going to be walking in the hills. The contours, the tracks, the trig points, the rivers, all give an almost tangible experience before you even take the first step. In a sense that's what a team needs – the ability not just to plan but to anticipate. We use 'roadmaps' a lot to extend the goal-setting process by inviting the team to map out what a certain period will look like, and what they need to have achieved at each 'way-mark'.

An example of a roadmap setting process

A global safety team had come together in the US to align around a vision for its future contribution to the business. We had used A4 size pictures to stimulate their thinking as to what this future will look like, which they were so keen to create. This constituted a vision setting process. The timescale was five years. Once this vision was clear and had been articulated in words, it was then easier to invite them to break the next five years up and articulate what they needed to achieve in each one towards the vision. We then entered the land of a thousand post-its with a busy afternoon populating each of the years. Standing back and looking at the roadmap was a highly satisfying and energizing process, unified and aligned the team around a big-picture goal (an objective in OKR terms), and key milestones, which were measurable.

Roadmap process: wisdom with hindsight

Purpose: This process helps both set a future destination in the form of a vision and create a roadmap for its achievement. These roadmaps can be used very flexibly, alongside OKRs, as well as following longer-term vision setting.

Figure 9.2 Roadmap Example

A Learning Organization Roadmap

End 2018: Global organizational learning community of practice established; develop a new narrative that Team speaks from; define the initial learning tools suite; Team commits to becoming a learning organization; learning organization maturity scale developed and Departments baselined on the scale.

End 2019: Global team introduced to organizational learning concepts; essential elements of the principles; All Leaders support and understand LO principles; redefine safety success; effective global learning through actionable shared learning (step change); organizational town hall safety meetings refer to organizational learning concepts; introduce LO to next level Leaders

End 2020: Step change in sharing global learning; pilot learning tools/methods; examples of different organizational learning tools are demonstrated and shared; LO principles form part of the business effectiveness scorecard; contractors leaders introduced to LO; LO actively and visibly supported by Leadership; dedicated resource in each Department for LO

End 2021: Global Leadership Team demonstrates Learning Behaviours consistently for situations Learning organization introduction to mid level of organization Learning organization in Corporate Management (audits, risk, etc.)

End 2022 (5 years): Learning embedded in company values; This is a learning organization; known for/as a model of LO business; Learning organizations is embedded in contractors LO principles included in global contracts

Process:

- Spread series of pictures – maybe 100 – around the floor and tables of work-shop room.
- Invite team members to select one or two pictures that depict for them the picture of success that they are seeking to create.
- You may also invite them to select another one or two pictures that depict where they are now in relation to that outcome.
- One by one they share their pictures and describe what the pictures mean to them and how they are a vision of success. The rest of the team is invited to listen carefully and as each person shares, to notice the patterns that are being articulated.
- Once everybody has placed their pictures on a convenient wall, the team stands back and is invited to share the key themes that emerged; these are noted down on post-its in order to capture the vision.
- The same process can be followed to capture the current state.
- Once done, and possibly using the same wall, you can break the space between the current and future state into periods – years, months, whatever makes sense.
- Then invite the team to imagine that the vision has already come true, and they are now looking back at the key things that they achieved in each of the periods to that point. What were those key actions and results at each point in time?
- With post-its in hand they can start populating those milestones.
- Often in a team workshop this then needs to be taken away and finalized by a smaller group and confirmed to the team soon after.

In setting direction, what about taking account of risk?

Interestingly this process can be adjusted to include consideration of antici-pated challenges, barriers, or indeed 'critical success factors'. Introducing anticipation of this kind is, for our money, useful. As a team coach it may well be that the organization is seeking to minimize risk, for instance in a safety environment. And yet if one focuses on risk alone it can be difficult to be inno-vative. So, a balance needs to be struck – every team and organization is differ-ent and occasionally needs to be challenged. I would, however, encourage consideration of risk, as described in our section on innovation – if you know it's coming, it's easier to prepare yourself and plan accordingly.

Roles

The importance of agreeing roles and of role clarity

Whatever label your role might have, it often entails a variety of goals and activ-ities that relate both to task as well as the management of relationships and processes. Very often, of course, it will involve the instigation and the leadership of change, and that change will necessitate engagement with others beyond the team, including one's peers. In these situations, one may be accountable, though not in direct control of resources, adding an interesting turn to your role.

In addition, a role can be taken to mean your unspoken contribution to the team – the role you play in team conversations, in problem-solving, in the human elements of the team's work. This is likely to be more related to your personality – traits (which are deemed to be more fixed as a function of genetics and upbringing) and preferences (which are deemed to be more malleable). We shall look at the latter in the 'use of difference' section later on in this chapter.

What cuts across many of these different kinds of definition of roles is the process of role negotiation. This is a process that can be used with teams whether they are seeking to refresh and reconfirm their roles, or whether they are new together, just signing up for a new goal set. It also has the powerful benefit of reinforcing what we described earlier as 'felt interdependence'. That is to say, the degree to which team members feel they need to rely on each other to complete their tasks. The more one can reinforce felt interdependence by agreeing common goals connected to individual ones, and then negotiate how you will work together to achieve your common goals, the more you will be operating as a team.

Gaining role clarity through role negotiation

Often, team members have expectations that are unclear to them and to others and may feel anxious about raising the issue without hurting their colleagues' feelings. Yet if expectations can be clarified and agreement struck on the 'exchange' between team members, it can be enormously helpful in getting things done and making team work more enjoyable. Team members can assist each other in delivering the work and in a way that they each find helpful. It actively builds trust and trustworthiness. Originally developed by Roger Harrison, a leading organizational psychologist, role negotiation is a way of stimulating interdependent activity in a team.

Vignette: The senior team of a major national charity had assembled for a day and a half to examine and recommit to a new goal set and agree how they would work together to deliver. We gave team members an opportunity to prepare themselves for role negotiation, which they had never carried out before. We then gave them a good chunk of time each in pairs, rotating them each around the team. The whole team completed the process within an afternoon. The CEO reported that the process was a revelation, an opportunity to re-balance not just relationships but refresh the team;s focus on the actions it needed to reach its goals, and revisit expectations of each other.

These are the preconditions for effective role negotiation:

- Both parties are willing to change their behaviour and activity and commit to specific action.
- Agreements need to be two-way, and felt to be fair by both parties.

- All agreements must be written down and a follow-up process and timeline agreed.
- Threats or pressures are unacceptable.
- It focuses on tasks, actions and behaviours.

Purpose of role negotiation: To agree, specifically, what each team member will do to contribute to the priorities of other team members and the team 'system', in service of the team task, and how they will go about those activities.

Process of role negotiation: This can work well both in a team workshop or on a one-to-one basis . . .

Preparation

Consider your own role – key goals and priorities. Prepare to share that.

For each of your colleagues, consider what they do that you **value**; what **requests** you have of them that would help you achieve your tasks; the **offers** you can make to them that you believe would assist them. Write them down.

Role negotiation

Set aside time with a colleague to 'negotiate' your roles and strike agreements. 30–40 minutes is usually enough for you both to share your prepared sheets and to negotiate to agreement. Once agreement is struck, write it down, again, using the sheet. Only agree to things that you are committed to doing. Be specific on what you are agreeing to do and when.

Follow-up

With your colleagues, check the agreements are working. Renegotiate if required. Import experiences into a team workshop, using process for a second round if required.

The actual conversation

- Each describe how you see your role, your goals and current priorities, in each of the systems you serve or lead: What is your role in service of this system?
- Then share your thinking.
  - Value: I value you doing . . . (so keep doing that)
  - Request: I would like you to change this . . .
  - Offer: I will do . . .
- Hear from them and start your 'negotiation'.
- Agree next steps with your colleague – what you will do for them and what they will do for you.

- Write the agreements down on the record sheet, retaining it for future reference (adapted from Harrison 1971).

Role negotiation can be used in a workshop setting, with preparation having been done prior to the workshop if possible. The timing can be adjusted to suit; teams that are very used to this process can run more swiftly than those who have just been introduced to it. The other variable, of course, is how much adjustment and re-balancing the team needs to do both in its dynamic as well as the arrangement of task and mutual support for delivery.

Vignette: For some time now, we have been working with the management team of a leading digital marketing agency. The early task was to develop teamship at the top, and part of that process was to introduce them to role negotiation. They were struck with the idea that, at a senior level, roles are a 'negotiated act', and ever since then role negotiation has been part of their language for adjusting relationships and task orientation. As a result, they can be found in bi-laterals renegotiating with just one colleague or triggering team renegotiation with everybody involved. Their familiarity with the process makes it a simple and powerful habit and one that has kept them focused in times of challenge as well as times of success, allowing them to break new ground as a business.

Accountability

What is accountability?

'Accountability refers to the implicit or explicit expectation that one may be called upon to justify one's beliefs, feelings, and actions to others' (Lerner and Tetlock 1999).

Accountability is intended to stimulate performance by focusing attention on those areas that will receive interest from others. However, the field of study is complex and research on accountability is not as advanced as organizational situations may require it to be. The positive effects of accountability are not guaranteed. To bring this to life, let's have a look at why it is important.

Why is it important? A look at accountability in matrix organizations

Accountability is important because it has a material impact on performance. Those who are held accountable are more likely to make things happen, and ensure that if things go wrong, there is somebody to come to. As I have observed earlier, many of us are in many teams in modern organizations – and now in matrix organizations where the prize for the organization is greater and more effective collaboration.

Bazigos and Harter (2016) highlight a recent Gallup poll that described 84 per cent of US employees as being in a matrix organization to some extent; 49 per cent served on multiple teams in any given day; 17 per cent of employees reported being in a 'super-matrix' where their managers reported to different people in their work with different teams. The research does confirm that employees reported more collaboration in matrix organizations, which one assumes is the purpose in part of creating a matrix structure. Bazigos and Harter go on to describe that 'organisations can mitigate the complexity associated with matrices through clear accountability and targets for individuals' (Bazigos and Harter 2016, 1). The original commentators on matrix organizations, Bartlett and Ghoshal (1991), described putting in the structures of a matrix as relatively easy. Making it work through the development of what they described as 'a healthy organizational psychology – the shared norms, values, and beliefs that shape the way individual managers think and act' is much more difficult, though for them ultimately beneficial.

Accountability occurs at different levels – everyone is accountable to contribute to the organization's goals, they take precedence over a team's goals, and they in turn take precedence over individual goals. One, of course, hopes that there is good alignment between each layer. I mention it here though because it is useful to consider the situation in which a team commits to a changing culture and greater collaboration between departments. In addition, individual leaders retain accountability for goals for which they may not retain all resources for delivery – some of those resources may lie outside their direct control, in other teams and in other parts of the organization. Is the culture change goal the imperative, or is it the delivery of the individual's goals for which they are accountable? Clearly, it is both and therefore change needs to occur in the way the individual leader delivers on those accountabilities. Like cars in an increasingly pedestrianized city centre, leaders will need to be good at negotiating and influencing to stay on track (and not get run over).

Only one person should be truly accountable for delivery of an outcome or indeed a process. That person may well be the final sign-off for more significant decisions, or the acquisition of more substantial resource or indeed the provision of influence and enrolment of others in the organization who can make a material difference to those who are responsible and working on the tasks. The single point of accountability re-enforces the (hopefully) positive aspects of accountability, principally that of ownership.

What of responsibility?

Responsibility, on the other hand, lies with those who contribute directly to the achievement of goals by delivering on the tasks. There may be many who were officially responsible for contributing to a particular goal or objective. Those who are responsible may also be able to make decisions and enrol additional resource to be able to make their contribution. This is not to be confused with the internally generated feeling of responsibility – which may pervade the experience of many in the leadership team, though they may not be officially 'responsible' for the tasks.

So, in two small examples, I may be accountable for the culture change programme, though others are responsible for its delivery. I may be accountable for 'zero harm' on my site, though my team leaders are responsible for delivering that outcome.

And, finally, to mutual accountability in a team

Mutual accountability is often absent particularly early on in the team's life. This may be for the same reason that accountability is often felt to be difficult – team members don't see it as their place, they may not know how to do it, they may feel they don't know enough about their colleague's area of work to be able to do it well. Yet mutual accountability is a hallmark of effective teamship. It is the sign that the leader has ceded some of their authority to all team members. Team members, for their part, feel that if one person fails, they all fail; if one needs help, then it should be forthcoming.

Mutual accountability is simply an extension of individual accountability. It can be defined as a mutual agreement to evaluate each other's progress towards achieving team goals. It includes activities such as determining support that is needed, challenge that may be required and helpful, and support for growing the accountable leader's capacity to deliver. It can be a formal or informal process and, in the best teams, mutual accountability is pro-actively applied, before progress appears to slip.

When coaching a team, it is important to check that the team has established sufficient psychological safety to hold each other to account in this way and have built relationships of trust such that the intention in the support and challenge process will be appropriate and understood by all. In addition, it is useful for the leader to continue to play their active role in accountability – holding individual team members to account as part of the normal process of governance, and holding the team to account for mutual decision-making, problem-solving and, of course, mutual accountability.

The more a team therefore can see the work of colleagues as contributing to their own and offer challenge and support to uphold the delivery of team goals, the more mutual accountability will be a useful contributor to performance. This, of course, assumes that team members are able to build effective relationships of trust and respect and that the climate in the team is one of safety. More on that later.

Decision-making

As has already been articulated in the chapter on team leadership, the more the team leader can encourage the team to solve problems together, the more cohesiveness the team will create and the more it will grow its collective capacity to deliver. The leader may also have a view as to which decisions are team decisions, which are individual decisions relating to particular functions or roles within the team, and which are decisions only they can make; it may also be true that the leader is charged with making the decisions yet wants input from the team on which decision they should make. Here we examine useful considerations in team decision-making.

Pitfalls in the team decision-making process

- The leader invites the team to make a decision and yet wrests back control being frustrated by the process.
- The team is invited to make the decision and yet polarizes around differences and 'locks out'.
- The team is charged with making the decision and yet nobody wants to disagree with the leader/the most influential team member.
- The team makes a decision that facts later reveal needs to be changed but their commitment continues.

Resolutions to these pitfalls

- Be clear on who is ultimately going to be making the decision – be it the team, the leader, or the leader informed by consultation with the team – and avoid changing tack on this or taking responsibility from the team once given.
- Collectively be clear on what the decision is about or the problem to be solved – create a shared view or shared 'mental model'. (A mental model is a 'schema', a way of looking at something that has been internalized through experience.)
- Make it safe for people to disagree – by holding the structure of the process and promote minority views even if they come from individuals who are not seen as expert in the subject.
- Invite questions to be posed and assumptions or 'workings' shown across the team, not just at the instigation of the coach or leader.
- Make it okay to fail and encourage learning from failure by engendering a tone of inquiry and curiosity vs taking a right/wrong position.
- Use simple processes by which decisions can be made or problems resolved, and solutions determined that are transparent.

Vignette: One of the teams that I studied, an asset leadership team for oil and gas platforms in the North Sea, was grappling with a particular problem that proved to be a challenge to solve. A number of attempts had been made. Time was ticking on. The coach who was working with them saw the opportunity to invite the team to a two-day session off-site. Immersion in the nature of the problem and building relationships such that barriers came down and creativity ensued, ensured that a lasting solution was found. It transpired that previous attempts had not really bottomed out what the problem was, so any solution when you look back transpired to be guesswork. A shared mental model was created in the team of the problem to be solved, the coach created sufficient psychological safety that encouraged contribution, and the team was able to create a variety of strategies that they could put in place and learn from, which they did. They had overcome the pitfalls.

Decision-making processes and following interest

There are many different decision-making processes that one can deploy as a coach and leader, and you may have your favourites. All of them in one way or another seek to solve problems, capitalize on opportunities or answer questions that have emerged for the team.

A most useful and simple way for a coach and a leader to support a decision-making process with some or all of the team is the concept of an hourglass. When coaching, one seeks to 'follow the interest' of an individual leader within agreed boundaries set by the goals of the process. This is true of coaching a team, of course, too. Yet each conversation with an individual and team follows a similar pattern: expansion and focus, expansion and focus. By expansion I mean inviting relevant information and data to be shared or possibilities to be explored and then at the point of focus the invitation is to choose either a singular path or to carry forward a number of ideas. This focus can then itself be expanded in the next part of the conversation. This helps all parties navigate the conversation and see if it needs to be expanded or focused. This both helps manage the process and the time taken for it, as well as participation – one can notice whether the expansion has allowed sufficient voice to be given to different opinions and different individuals, and where the decision for focus has come from and whether that's appropriate.

Hourglass example: The leadership team needed to induct several groupings of multidisciplinary teams who would be responsible for specific end-to-end processes within the business. This was a new way of working, so starting off on the right foot felt important to the team. We worked with the team to identify all of the different possibilities as to how they might induct and then support those teams (expand). We then asked them which they were interested in pursuing. They made their selection (focus) and we then expanded each of those ideas (expand) until they had a sufficient degree of clarity as to how they would take induction forward (focus).

An adjusted RACI

In an effort to clarify the decision-making protocol and ensure clarity of roles in pursuing particular decisions, many teams use the RACI (Responsibility, Accountability, Consulted, Informed) approach. When working with our teams and clients we prefer to make an adjustment to this process.

Vignette: We worked with two teams to help them create joint goals for the next period. One team was the client, the other team was the contractor – both were keen on creating a partnership approach to their work together. There had been a lot of tension between the two teams and the goals they agreed upon; ways of not just resolving the conflict but focusing on outcomes important to both teams. Once the goals were set, they then worked to ensure that

Figure 9.3 Managing the breadth and depth of the team conversation

each of the five goals had defined roles against them, against which they could track their progress, and within which they could solve problems together. We used the structure below to help them be clear, particularly on the distinction between accountability and responsibility.

Role description

- **Accountable:** 'The bucks stops here . . .'. Only one person is accountable.
- **Responsible:** 'I am directly involved in making this happen . . .'. This may be the same person as the one who is accountable; there may be many who are responsible.
- **Consulted:** 'I need to be involved so talk with me . . .'. Brings expertise or experience and may exert a veto.
- **Informed:** 'Keep me posted . . .'. Someone on the official distribution list.

The team as a resource for decision-making

As described earlier in the section on before you start coaching the team, the team leader may at times view the team as a resource for them to make a decision. If the decision-making process starts with that being clear, with a simple process to guide the conversation, team decision-making is enhanced. This borrows from a number of settings including a medical setting. Here, multidisciplinary teams of senior and trainee doctors and nursing staff make decisions on patient care in 'decision rounds'. These rounds are frequent and regular. They draw upon the resources of all those present. The person making the decision may be the senior doctor or they may delegate that to a junior doctor under their supervision, who, along with their colleagues the nurses, have greater knowledge of specific patients (Reader et al., in Salas et al. 2005).

It's useful to remember that the same model can be used for any member of the team. If a team member requires the resources of the team, they may set up a conversation that appoints their colleagues as a resource for their own decision. That decision affects everybody in the team but that one team member is either directly accountable or instrumental in delivery in some way. Extending this principle, we use what we call consultancy circles. These are where the team acts as a resource for each team member by turn. The structure can be decided on by the coach, the leader, or the team, as can the timing. What is useful is to ask the team to practise their ability to ask questions, to listen, and to raise challenges to their colleague as they support the decision-making. This mirrors the kinds of process in a learning set, though develops the team at the same time.

Vignette: In coaching a client, my colleagues supported the team to arrive at its own decision-making protocol. This made the team meetings more focused, preparation for them productive, and the decision-making itself much easier and quicker:

- Clarity on whether this is a team or a departmental decision – together with clarity in advance of what you want input on (for Information, Consultation, Co-ordination or Decision).
- Clarity on *what* the decision is about. (What is the problem we are trying to solve?)
- It's fine if it's not democratic – let it just be clear.
- If there is disagreement – the team leader will act as the deadlock breaker.
- Disagree if you need to – but once the decision is made – fully commit and follow through once you have made the decision – clarity on expectations/ consequences of what will happen next (owners and timelines!).

Innovation

Increasingly, teams are required to be innovative, to reinvent, to adapt and think beyond the current, the accepted, the 'normal'. This might be because they need to do more with less or create a completely new way of operating or delivering on their purpose, or even a completely new product or service. Innovation is increasingly, then, on every team's agenda.

It is increasingly the aspiration of many organizations to accelerate the process of innovation. They see a bottom-line advantage in doing so, which is supported by the evidence. A recent study in the US concluded that organizations that had a system for innovating fared better in sales growth and profitability. It pays to invest and to innovate. Leadership teams are increasingly expected to lead this acceleration as well as to demonstrate it in the way that they tackle problems, make decisions and organize their operation. It is no longer just the preserve of the innovation department to innovate. I talked to my good friend and fellow coach Philip Oliver of Eureka!Europe, to discuss what teams can do to accelerate innovation and how coaches and leaders can support this to occur. This section is the product of that conversation. There is much here to support team fundamentals being in place, which then create the foundation from which the team can innovate.

What is innovation in a team context?

Irrespective of the context, innovation is about producing something that people want that is 'meaningfully unique'. It is meaningful to the three parties involved – to you, to your organization and importantly to the client or customer. And it's unique insofar as the features and characteristics that it offers have an element of newness and difference. That sounds very subjective, but there are ways of measuring 'meaningful uniqueness'. It is important that a leader and their team share a common understanding of, and belief in, the idea, or else they are unlikely to support and advance the project.

How is this different from problem-solving?

Innovation is a class of problem-solving. Much of bringing an idea to life commercially will involve problem-solving. However, innovation is about creating value, and not just trying to overcome blockers and challenges. It has a productive objective behind it, a commercial goal.

We make a distinction between continuous business improvement at one end of the scale, and pure innovation – bringing to life something new – at the other end. Our definition of innovation covers the whole spectrum.

Vignette: A leadership team in a utility with whom we worked were seeking to meet nearly 1,000 challenges in an innovative manner, which did not just solve customer problems, but created value for all parties. They created the idea of 'not pouring concrete', not digging holes. This is because there were often simpler and less destructive and costly solutions that involved either technology or an innovative way of working. Despite the fact that it was doing less, it created value, and in some cases, significant longevity of solution. Their costs would be significantly reduced over time from this approach.

A useful equation: 'Meaningful uniqueness' (or MU, in Eureka!Europe shorthand) is not just a working definition but also a way of explaining the key organizational, psychological and behavioural levers for generating truly innovative ideas. Specifically, the ability to develop MU ideas is a function of external stimulus, leveraged by the degree of diversity of thinking and experience applied, and is diminished by the amount of fear that exists in the system. Let's unpack this, using the innovation equation below to illustrate this from the perspective of a team leader.

Figure 9.4 The Innovation Equation
With permission, Doug Hall, Innovation and Engineering

The team will not have 'big and bold' ideas, that can be operationalized and commercialized, unless the **diversity** in that team has been productively engaged. This is about harnessing the team's diversity of thinking, expertise and experience. The **stimulus** we're speaking of is effectively the creative driver. Very often this stimulus comes from outside the team, or perhaps entirely from outside the organization (e.g. open innovation). The **fear** in this equation might manifest in statements like: 'I'm fearful (in this context) of the team'; 'I'm fearful of speaking up and if I say something that is slightly unusual or if I speak my mind a little too much that's not a good thing'. If the wider organization doesn't accept fresh ideas readily it discourages team members from proactively finding better ways of doing what they do or inventing truly 'new and different' products.

So, what are the other challenges in innovating in a team?

These fall into two categories: people and process.

People problems

- **Fear:** We have spoken about this above.
- **Ownership:** 'I don't know that I have permission to think differently and to bring my contributions to the table.'

- **Skills:** 'I know you want me to do this, but I don't have the tools, though I may have the creativity.'
- **Culture:** The leader of the team doesn't tolerate failure. If we don't feel we can fail, then we don't feel free to experiment.
- **Leadership:** The leader doesn't display their own fallibility by admitting that they need help ('diversity is helpful to us'), that they don't have all the answers ('stimulus brings fresh insights'), and that it's OK to make mistakes as long as we're learning ('failure is part of learning and experimentation').
- Wider culture in the organization.

Process problems

- **Problems of value and measuring value:** We take action, but the results of the action are not quantified or quantifiable.
- **Alignment:** We are busy doing something great in our team. Unfortunately, none of that aligns with what either the department or the wider organization really wants from us; and which in the longer term brings into question the viability of the team.
- **Workflow (the way in which work is done):** A fairly obvious thing that impacts your ability to innovate – the team cannot be innovative if it doesn't have a way of innovating consistently. It is the very inconsistency that makes it hit or miss, and the very hit or miss nature that then reduces the value to the client or the other departments it's working with to improve the business; people can't rely on the team to deliver what is required.
- **Tools and systems:** Without having the tools to hand that support the full range of the create–communicate–commercialize innovation process, it makes it really difficult to get the job done, meaning the team is unable to meet its commitments.

And what are the enablers for innovation in a team?

- **Alignment:** An enormous enabler is alignment – from sponsor level to innovation leader level to innovation practitioner level. Any team involved in innovating or upgrading internal processes needs to understand and agree the 'mission' they have committed to, including an understanding of the constraints and 'no go' areas for the project.
- **Leadership:** It is a fundamental requirement of the leader of the team to recognize that failure to innovate is, in the first instance, overwhelmingly likely to be down to the 'system' (including the team) in which people are working, rather than the individuals themselves. For this we have W. Edwards Deming to thank, whose research established the principle that 6 per cent of problems may be ascribed to the worker, and 94 per cent to the system in focus. The leader of the team has the responsibility to act on the system to the extent they can, on behalf of the team, in order to enable innovation to thrive.

- **Provision of development:** If the leader is asking the team to amplify its creativity, then ensuring it has the tools and techniques is critical. This ensures that it can consistently and reliably engage with the task in an innovative way.
- **Role modelling and psychological safety:** It is the leader's responsibility to role model creating the safe space and therefore to say: 'I don't know; I don't have all the answers; I fail a lot and I need help'. This language and behaviour nurtures a culture of innovation within the team.
- **Leadership encouragement to solve problems together:** It's the leader's job to encourage people to be creative and problem-solve. Agreeing the boundaries within which innovation can occur and clarifying the outcome is time well spent.

Why is innovation important for a team at this time?

A recent article in the *Scotsman* (September 2020) noted that the small and medium enterprises of the UK are going to be the organizations on which the route to recovery will depend. Those organizations will need teams with extreme flexibility, with the ability to reinvent themselves – to 'pivot'. That's not going to happen without having teams that are capable of innovating, and it's not just the guys in the back room – the five people who the organization has chosen to 'be innovative'. It's leveraging the diversity of the whole organization and creating a culture that engenders innovative thinking. It is essential.

What is the cost of poor innovation to the team and the organization?

Apart from the obvious financial or reputational implications for the organization, one of the biggest costs is a hidden one: disengagement. If I ask you to contribute your ideas as I should do, but I'm not creating an enabling environment, it's enormously frustrating; or if I'm contributing ideas and the organization doesn't do anything with those ideas, it triggers the antibiotic resistance effect: if you run creativity 'hackathons' too many times without having a way to make the ideas come alive, people will eventually become despondent and withhold contribution.

How much should the team focus on risks in seeking to innovative? What about team learning and innovation?

One of the fears that either the leader or the team members will experience is the fear of failure, but also the pressure of trying to deliver. Better to have the recognition that there are risks in trying anything different, and in particular anything new. The approach that we would advocate is 'fail fast, fail cheap'. This sounds trite but is actually very pragmatic and helpful. The traditional approach is that you make a long list of those risks, you rank them according to their various relative scores, you stick them under the nose of some review committee and you meet once a month to mitigate some of the risks. Studies show that most projects going through a project governance process will lose up to 50 per cent of the value of an innovation with something that started out as a great idea. A powerful idea ends up being atrophied and becoming a poor shadow of its former self.

Fail fast, fail cheap is different. It says just accept that innovation is a risky endeavour. Put your biggest risk on the table, then do everything you can to take that risk out of the game. That is to say, go and try something, learn more about that risk in reality (test your assumptions), and continue in this manner until you take the risk right out of the equation if you can. Once you've done that with your biggest risk, move down the list to the next one; but do it at pace and with intentionality. This allows you to collect data that will guide how you should move forward. You quickly get to a point where the risks are much diminished, or at least at a level that you can work with. You will have learned a lot along the way and have de-risked the project at the same time. The work our colleagues have done at the Innovation Engineering Institute demonstrates that this 'fail fast, fail cheap' approach, when applied in a systematic way, can add up to 23 per cent to the value of the initial idea; rather than weakening the idea, the process makes it stronger. A team collaborating in this way can really accelerate innovation and problem-solving.

Use of difference

Making good use of difference

We can all talk a very good game about how much we welcome the difference that others bring – by helping our thinking, stimulating new debates, and arriving at better solutions. It seems a brilliant idea. Good perhaps, right up to the point where we disagree with a team member who expresses a difference of opinion or of habit, and you either do not have the depth of relationship or trust required, or the in-the-moment ideas as to how to retain an open mind. However, 'differences' between people in the team are still very helpful.

Given the benefit that diversity brings, it is worth investing the time and effort required by both the team leader and team members, to uncover and make best use of the diversity that exists in the team. This section is about harvesting the good the diversity brings and minimizing the challenges.

Diversity, inclusion and bias

For many years much has been talked about on the subject of diversity. The science on teams is pretty clear. Diversity of team membership is important for team success. If diversity meets the basic requirements of skill and experience required by the team's tasks, then diversity makes a substantial contribution to the quality of decisions that a team makes and therefore the outcome the team creates. This book is not about the practical and cultural challenges of ensuring a diverse workforce; however, the fact is that teams are a microcosm of organizations and being able to work with difference well can contribute significantly to team performance.

What do we mean by diversity?

There are many dimensions of diversity, of course. Here are some – there is a diversity in personality – in basic traits, as well as preferences, diversity of experiences, diversity of ethnicity, gender, disability, neurodiversity. No one wishes to be in a team where diversity is an end in itself. However, it remains the scientific case that greater diversity does, all other things being equal, create better teams.

> Diversity in nationality and ethnicity creates better solutions and makes for better decisions . . . diversity in knowledge, educational profile and position has the same effect, though . . . this depends on individual team members being prepared to listen and be open to the ideas of others. (Kandola 2009)

This brings us to inclusion. Inclusion is 'the degree to which individuals feel part of critical organisational processes' (Mor-Barak and Cherin 1998). We have worked with teams where some team members do not feel included, which makes us think about those who are being led by the team – how do they feel? As always, it starts from the top and emanates from the behaviours of the leaders. If team members do not feel included themselves, it will affect how they think and feel about the team and their work – it will affect the dynamic of the team. In an Adaptable Team where all things are 'connected' one cannot escape the consequences. If the team climate includes team members feeling safe, if they experience sufficient trust and if they feel they can speak up, they will feel included.

Unconscious bias

Finally, unconscious bias affects us all. This is 'any detectable bias in our attitudes or behaviour that operates outside of our awareness. It could be asking a man rather than a woman to pitch a project because, subconsciously, you presume he will be more confident and assertive' (Dr Keon West, social psychologist, in Kandola 2009).

There are over 150 categories of unconscious bias, and here are our top six, which are particularly relevant to team coaching:

- **Affinity bias:** Preference for people who share the same qualities as you or someone you like.
- **Conformity bias:** Influenced unduly by others.
- **Conformation bias:** The primary search for evidence that backs up your opinions.
- **Gender bias:** A preference for one gender over another in context – rooted in gender roles and stereotypes.

- **Halo effect:** Focus on one great feature about someone.
- **Horn effect:** Focus on one less good feature about someone.

Raising a team's awareness as to the biases at play in their leadership of others or in their relationships within the team may be crucial to the team's ability to sustain results over time and lead effectively.

A focus on differences in personality: a preference-based approach

We shall focus now on the differences that individuals display in the way in which they prefer to operate and the contributions they prefer to make to a team. We choose a preferences route rather than a trait-based route because we find it to be a more accessible way for team members to think about differences in personality and how that affects the team – both in terms of its relationships and its approach to task.

An example of one difference that can emerge in a team is between those who are more introverted and those who are more extroverted. It is one of the agreed dimensions of personality in many psychometric assessments. Someone who is more introvert will prefer to think things through before speaking, may be quieter at meetings, prefer time to prepare and think things through before contributing. Someone who is more extrovert will prefer to talk things out to understand them, can be impulsive and is likely to contribute a lot at meetings. If this is understood, knowing how to create a balanced conversation in a team meeting, gain the best contributions from all and ensure good preparation for those who need it, becomes easier for the team. This is one example of many.

The instrument that we use most often is the Team Management Profile (TMP). The TMP was developed by psychologists Margerison and McCann seeking an answer to the question 'what makes teams successful?' Their research yielded a clear view of what work in a team required at each stage of the task life cycle. They then matched these eight different activities overlaid with four different individual preferences and created the Team Management Wheel – indicative of how people prefer to operate at work in a team. The attractiveness of the approach to us is that it is focused on team activity at work, and the reports are valid and reflect individual preferences.

It is used to understand how team members prefer to take up their roles and perform tasks and indeed the kinds of tasks they are most attracted to. This allows the team to ensure that all of the different parts of the team's work is being attended to – for instance, in gathering data from outside the team, for monitoring progress, for planning and execution.

The TMP displays team members' role preferences on a 'Team Management Wheel', which shows all eight possible roles. Once the team has been created, the leader and coach work with what they find, supporting the team to identify and use the differences to achieve the goals.

Differences in power and supporting their appropriate use

Team members can also differ in the power they have. The un-self-aware use of this power can have a destabilizing effect on the team but it's appropriate use can be extremely helpful. Being able to sense when power is being displayed and whether it's helpful or unhelpful for the team is very useful to the coach and the leader. Power is the capacity to influence the attitudes and behaviour of others. This is distinct from authority where individuals are vested with the right to influence others.

Power dynamics in a team can show itself up in a variety of different ways. Consider the power that operational team members have over those who are in the support function, those who lead a large number of people who may be felt to have greater power than those who lead a smaller number, men who may be deemed to have more power than women, extroverts who may be felt to have more power than those who are more introverted.

Personal power is when a team member has the power to influence others either because they are an expert in a particular field that is required for team functioning or because they have built good relationships and are respected and trusted. Clearly, an individual leader can have personal power from expertise or respect. Positional power is retained because the team member has control over resources, rewards, sanctions or information. While positional power may be important for the administration of the team, applying it appropriately is also important. The retention and use of these kinds of power rests largely on the degree to which they are applied with respect, transparency and authenticity as well as integrity. They rely therefore on the character of the team member.

Both individual and group power and differences between individuals in exercising their power therefore are both important to be aware of and to encourage the team to use wisely. If there are genuine and legitimate reasons why one party has more power than another, then transparency is critical. This may well be the case in the leader's role in making final decisions for instance, or the head of function making the final decision on issues that affect their discipline. The danger lies in the team saying that there is equality and then manifestly not applying that equality. That will lead to a sense of inequity in the relationships and fear and anxiety can grow.

When difference in teams hits the buffers: conflict

The coach and the leader's role

It is part of the coach's and the leader's role to be able to examine or indeed help the team understand what kind of conflict is occurring in their team, and if there are unused strengths within the team they could deploy. If there is no conflict, it is also important to consider where that conflict is going to – are there conversations that are being had on the surface level, which may indicate a 'pseudo-team' is at play where team members are ignoring difference to keep the peace? Or is there no conflict because their interdependence as a team has not been re-enforced?

The impact of conflict can be huge. The CBI (*Personnel Today* 2017) estimated that it cost UK businesses £33 billion a year, takes up to 20 per cent of leadership time and potentially results in the loss of 370 million working days per annum. The impact on team members can also be huge. It can trigger sleepless nights, anxiety and depression. Knowing how to handle it therefore becomes a business imperative and a leadership and team responsibility.

What is conflict in a team?

Conflict is when there are 'real or perceived incompatible goals or interests' (De Wit et al. 2012). There are four kinds of conflict, all of which can be found in a team:

- **Task:** Disagreements about task content (De Wit et al. 2012; Jehn 1995)
- **Relationship:** Interpersonal incompatibilities and tensions (De Wit et al. 2012; Jehn 1995)
- **Process:** Disagreements about the logistics of task completion including roles, responsibilities, and work arrangements (Jehn 1995)
- **Status:** Disputes over members' relative positions of respect in the team's social hierarchy (Bendersky and Hayes 2012).

Task conflict can be valuable given that it reflects a diversity of opinion and the search for better strategies for delivery. Studies reveal that all other things being equal, task conflict aids team members' understanding of what is required and yields higher quality decisions and more creativity (Amason 1996). However, relationship conflict is consistently positively correlated with a negative impact on team performance. If relationship conflict co-exists with task conflict, the gains of team conflict are reduced or disappear. In addition, moods can worsen, and psychological consequences can accrue. Process conflict is 'reliably harmful in teams' on measures of group co-ordination, group performance and member satisfaction (De Wit et al. 2012; Behfar et al. 2011 in Salas et al. 2005).

Reduce the fear of the unknown

There are a number of ways in which we could look at conflict, and it is useful to consider our own response to the idea of conflict. Kilmann and Thomas (1977) propose that conflict is a 'difference in what is valued' (or seen as important). This takes the sting out of the emotional response that team members may have to conflict – which is often one of avoidance or conversely aggression. Often, unhelpful conflict can be avoided by reducing the fear of the unknown. When we know more about the assumptions that others make, their experiences that influence their thinking and the differences they bring in the way that they think, we are more likely to appreciate their input and to listen when they share.

Go towards the difference, do not get stuck

A question that we use in a whole variety of different circumstances is 'what do you know now that in the future you're going to have wished that you acted upon?' This question is very useful because it verbalizes those observations that are just beneath the surface, the felt sense we have as to how events may unfold. If you experience a colleague as difficult to work with, that may well be time for a 'crucial conversation' (Patterson et al. 2011). A crucial conversation is one in which there are opposing opinions, strong emotions and the stakes are high. In the book of the same name they describe situations in which one can become trapped either by being silent – withdrawing, avoiding the situation, covering it over, or being aggressive – seeking to control, label and attack, and all of these can be quite subtly enacted. Neither of which, of course, will resolve the situation. The authors encourage making the conversation safe to be had and then engaging in dialogue. In a team situation, psychological safety is crucial and we shall discuss this later.

Vignette: We worked with two teams who were in conflict with one another. One was the 'client' and the other was the 'contractor'. Despite the fact that they had at the start of the contract developed a partnership agreement, it appeared that both parties felt that it had been compromised. The meetings together had become highly contractual, where the invocation of penalties for non-compliance, and disappointment and anger were on the rise. In preparation we interviewed each member of both teams, both about their own team as well as how they experienced the other team. We created reports for both teams that included the feedback from the other team as well as what they said about themselves. Within a two-day workshop, we invited them to reflect on both reports and then partway through the first day asked them to share the feedback that they had for the other team verbally, in real time. The team on receipt of that feedback were then required to repeat back what they had heard and receive confirmation that what they heard had both been accurate as well as reflected the spirit of the feedback and its intention. We alternated one team to the next until all the feedback had been exhausted and each team felt heard. The teams then went back into their huddles and devised ways of addressing conflicts they were experiencing. A final plenary session on the first day allowed the teams to share how they experienced the process to that point and what they now thought was possible. Both teams had previously reached the 'violence' point in expression of the anger and disappointment they experienced, though some individuals early on remained silent and became visibly upset. However, once their voices had been heard and acknowledged and their feedback appreciated, the teams were fully able to move on and construct a different future, driving the real value from partnership that they both sought.

Support and challenge

Why challenge and support in a team?

To challenge and support each other in a team is a critical skill and activity for any team member. 'Pro-social behaviour', where a team member volunteers help in any form, contributes to the building of trust. Both challenge and support are helping behaviours. They are also, of course, critical skills for a team coach and a team leader. Given that all parties are human beings, it would not be too provocative to say that each has their own challenges to overcome in presenting a high order of healthy challenge in order that conversations can be as effective as possible. In our experience, one of the most important habits to build in a team is to raise the level of productive challenge – we notice it is often lacking, and teams tell us they need more of it. They are right – the more challenge in particular, the better the chance of the team making good decisions and embarking on co-ordinated action.

A way to look at challenge in a team: the challenge and rapport model

For years, we have used a very simple way of describing challenge. This is the challenge and rapport model.

First of all, let's define challenge: We define challenge as to test, to stretch, to invite another to compete, 'to step up', to think or do something that they might find difficult yet ultimately beneficial and rewarding.

What about the definition of rapport? We define rapport as a feeling of connection and momentary empathy between two or more parties where there is a sense of understanding and being understood. Rapport is different from trust, which takes longer to establish. Rapport can occur in moments.

Figure 9.5 The Challenge and Rapport Model

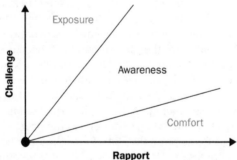

What is the aim of challenge?

The aim of challenge is to help your colleague or colleagues, or the client, adjust or transform their thoughts, feelings or behaviours such that it becomes ultimately more productive for them and for others and for the organization as a result.

In applying these definitions to the model, we see that there is an intimate relationship between the degree of challenge that can be bought to a conversation and the degree of rapport that one has with the subject of the challenge – whether you're a team member, team leader or team coach. If one has a high level of rapport with the subject of the challenge, then both parties can feel pretty comfortable. In that comfort there is not necessarily a huge amount of learning. There may be some, but it's not accelerated, and ideas are not shifted. By the same token, if there is a high level of challenge in the conversation, then the subject of the challenge can feel exposed, embarrassed, even shamed. This, of course, is not helpful for learning either because when one feels exposed one goes into defence, and shutdown. If, however, one can balance the connection with your colleague or client and increasingly offer a higher degree of challenge with that increasing level of rapport, then one can hit the sweet spot – the zone of awareness as we describe it. And in that zone the awareness that is created is not just about what is currently so, but also the possibilities that can be imagined, and then acted upon. Certainly, as a coach the more one can help the team to occupy the zone of awareness the better. An understanding as a coach, as to where you are, too, is incredibly helpful. We each have our own threshold for the level of challenge that we are prepared to offer and to accept. Understanding where those thresholds are and with whom, is incredibly useful. One may accept a challenge from one person but not another, but, of course, if you are the team coach you need to be the person that everybody can trust sufficiently to accept challenge from. This is founded on both rapport as well as trust. It is worth bearing in mind that T.S. Eliot is quoted as saying 'only those who will risk going too far can possibly find out how far one can go', so perhaps it is worth testing those thresholds once in a while.

What gets in the way of more challenge?

What stops people from challenging in the way we have been describing? We ask this question a lot in our workshops, and the response that we get, ultimately, is that individuals fear the loss of relationship, with the individual or with the team. One must remember, of course, that that fear resides in the potential giver of challenge, not necessarily in the mind of the receiver at all. So, both parties must work hard to maintain a good level of challenge, while the coach stays 'in touch', in rapport, with team members. That is not to confuse rapport with the desire to be liked or collude with the team.

An exercise for coaches and team members

This is for self-reflection or to be used in a team (in pairs) to accelerate the level of challenge:

- Who are you challenging now (in the team) and what is the impact?
- Who are you not challenging (in the team) and what are you avoiding?
- What might the team gain from your challenge?
- What is stopping you?
- How might you overcome what is stopping you?
- What specifically will you do? (Who, where, when, with what intention/ outcome)?

What are the targets of challenge in a team?

Each challenge is focused on a target. Table 9.1 shows the targets and some examples of them.

Table 9.1 Targets for challenge and some examples

Target	Example
Prejudice: An adverse judgement or opinion formed without knowledge or examination of the facts	Engineers do not express emotion
Self-limiting beliefs: Thoughts you see as 'the truth' that limit your ability or will to act	I cannot do this
Assumptions: A thing that is accepted as true or as certain to happen, without evidence	Safety is always about resources
Discrepancies: A lack of compatibility or similarity between two or more facts	The organization is going through a lot of change; it's nice to have a bit of stability for once in my life
Behaviour: The way in which one acts, especially towards others	I am sorry I have not had time to do this since our last session ... or excuse me while I answer that call ...
Predictable dishonesty (distortions, games, smoke screens)	My manager and I both have the same goals
Unused strengths and resources	I am not good at inspiring others (though you see them do so, or in a sense it is a hidden resource)

Useful tools and exercises

Tools in challenge: your challenge toolkit

It is useful to build your own toolkit for challenge to build the challenge habit. Figure 9.6 shows the principal tools that we recommend:
Here are some examples of each:

- **Call for data and evidence:** What evidence do you have for this?
- **Challenge the logic:** If you are saying this as well as this ... ?
- **Understanding hypothesis and theories:** What theory do you have here?
- **Giving feedback:** This is what I see ...
- **Checking consequence:** If you think in this way, what might be the useful and less useful consequences of that?

Figure 9.6 Your Challenge Toolkit

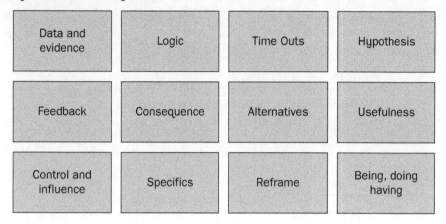

Data and evidence	Logic	Time Outs	Hypothesis
Feedback	Consequence	Alternatives	Usefulness
Control and influence	Specifics	Reframe	Being, doing having

- **Presenting or inviting alternative views:** What do others think or see here?
- **Checking for usefulness or utility:** How useful is that view?
- **Check for control and influence over outcomes:** What do you control or influence here?
- **Re-frame:** What if you looked at it like this?

Challenge focus: feedback

Beyond improving their listening and raising the level of challenge in the team, teams we work with often say that they do not receive enough feedback from each other. This is a critical micro skill within challenge – without it, we do not know how we are progressing or what others wish from us.

Feedback on tasks was found to have a significant effect on team productivity, improving it by 50 per cent (Pritchard et al. 1988) and a significant positive impact on learning (Thorndike 1927). Research on feedback has shown that the amount of affirmative feedback should exceed that of developmental feedback.

What is feedback?

Feedback can be defined as 'sharing how you experience another or others'. The purpose of feedback is to reduce the blind spots that we all have in order that there is more self-awareness available to make decisions that translate into superior performance. Blind spots are things that are known or can be observed by others but are not known to oneself. This may well then trigger disclosure to others of things that are not seen by them that you do know about, that may well be affecting performance. Both rely again on sufficient rapport and in this case a sufficient degree of trust, particularly in the intention of the feedback giver.

Figure 9.7 The CORN Feedback Process

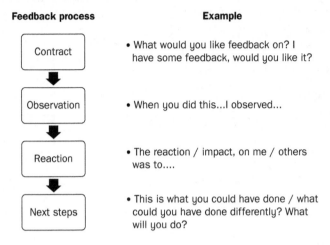

Feedback process	Example
Contract	• What would you like feedback on? I have some feedback, would you like it?
Observation	• When you did this...I observed...
Reaction	• The reaction / impact, on me / others was to....
Next steps	• This is what you could have done / what could you have done differently? What will you do?

Principles of useful feedback

This is a useful feedback 'Charter' from the research – feedback is more likely to be accepted if there is:

- Goal consensus (agreement as to what the intention is)
- Emphasis on appreciation
- Concrete and specific descriptions are used
- Constructive motives
- Not withheld especially if it is 'negative'
- Owned by the giver
- At the right time.

A feedback process

Figure 9.7 shows a useful feedback process to assist clarity when giving feedback, operating like a checklist.

Summary

We looked at seven fundamentals that team members need to be really good at with coaching support.

- Setting direction
  - Goal setting is 'among the most valid and practical theories of employee motivation in organisational psychology' (Locke and Latham 2002).

- o It works by directing the team's energy and activity towards the desired outcomes.
- o Goals need to be:
  - o Small in number so as not to be forgotten easily
  - o Challenging, thereby encouraging confidence
  - o Outcomes (not activities) – not a shopping list of actions
  - o Compelling in that they trigger the creative search for delivery strategies
  - o Important to stakeholders and to the team
  - o Aligned within and outside the team
  - o Not conflicting, avoiding turf wars
- o Roadmaps are a useful addition to traditional goal setting.
- Agreeing roles and developing accountability
  - o Being clear on one's role in a team is crucial and can usefully be achieved by a process of role negotiation – paired discussions around the team to build interdependence and bring clarity to the exchange between team members.
  - o Mutual accountability is a mutual agreement to evaluate each other's progress towards achieving team goals. This is a habit that high-performing teams engage in.
- Making sound decisions
  - o The team is an invaluable resource for decision-making, though there are pitfalls. These can be overcome by being clear on who is making the decisions and the role the team plays in that process, as well as building an enabling team culture where team members can fully participate.
- Innovating
  - o Teams are increasingly being required to be innovative, and produce outputs that are 'meaningfully unique'.
  - o This is more possible of the team in which team members feel it is safe to speak up and where there are the appropriate skills and processes in place.
- Making good use of difference
  - o Diversity, coupled with inclusion contributes to better decision-making and higher team performance.
  - o An awareness of cognitive bias in a team helps team members avoid unhelpful assumptions.
  - o Using preference-based psychometrics can be helpful for team members to understand dimensions of difference and use them effectively.
  - o Where there is conflict determining the nature of that conflict and knowing how to use or diffuse it is important.
- Supporting and challenging
  - o These are important skills for coach and team members alike where the challenge / rapport model is helpful in overcoming the anxiety in challenge and building effective team interaction.

10 Team dynamic

Make or break

The health of the team dynamic will make or break the team. Though just beneath the surface and ever present, it does not need to be feared and cannot be ignored. It is not an accident that when discussing team dynamics, the words healthy or unhealthy are used. A healthy team dynamic has a critical role to play in keeping team members healthy both physically and psychologically. It can also play a huge part in ensuring the team takes effective and coordinated action to generate sustainable results.

While on paper a good team and a good dynamic looks easy to build, it almost always requires team understanding and effort to make it work. Here we examine what makes a healthy and productive team dynamic and ways in which it can be generated.

Introduction

What are team dynamics?

Teams are complex dynamic 'systems' and ones that are constantly changing and shifting. They are subject to the forces acting on them from outside (as we have spoken about), other parts of the system (however they might be defined), as well as the forces that lie within the team. Those dynamics are hidden from view. Their roots may be in tangible form – from hierarchy that relates to job title, from different amounts of experience and skill, different physical attributes of team members; or intangible – assumptions about others, interpretation of behaviour, beliefs about others. Dynamics are the hidden 'social forces and influences' (Lewin 1947) that drive an emotional response of togetherness, belonging, connection, trust and feeling safe or the opposite – feeling fearful, anxious, angry and unheard.

These forces are constantly changing through shifts in mood, emotion, situations, physical states and environment, too.

Why are they important?

In a team those thoughts and feelings drive actions. Actions drive results. If there is not an alignment between the results the team aims for, the nature of the actions required and the thoughts and feelings that enable a good quality of action, the team will not get good results.

Consider for a moment a team that is behind on its delivery targets, where the new leader is greeted with data that they can't trust, and team members experience meetings that are by turns terminally dull, and full of tension and frustration. Thoughts about how to solve the principal challenges the team faces are highly divergent and there never seems to be enough time to rest on one problem at a time and solve it. Team members give up and focus on their own patch, wanting to keep their heads down and avoid the heat. This team's ability to engage in fruitful decision-making and productive and coordinated action would be limited. Their thoughts and their feelings are not aligned with the quality of actions they need to engage in to create the results that they may well already have agreed. Their ability to work through an agreed priority of challenges, while exchanging views, and assumptions and drive to resolution and decision, is at a premium – and if they get it right without diving into relationship conflict and instead build team member understanding between each other, they will succeed. How people think and feel about the team, about its task, its objectives, as well as the other team members, and indeed the leader too, is highly material to the quality of the actions the team can sustain.

A healthy team dynamic is one in which the team members feel engaged with a meaningful task and with each other, and where they feel able to speak up and share, can trust each other and align around some simple expectations for which they hold themselves mutually accountable. The more team members can develop and sustain this dynamic, the more they will be able to stay connected, aligned and pulling in the same direction. So, a healthy dynamic requires that the team develops:

- **Sufficient trust:** Such that team members feel that they can rely on each other
- **Psychological safety:** Creating a safe environment where team members can speak up and solve problems together
- **Alignment** on how they will behave towards each other, connecting on what they see as important
- **Commitment and belief:** whether the team members feel they will be successful and whether they are committed to the team's endeavours.

Emotional contagion

Before we look at each of the above, a brief look at emotional contagion. I can't be the only one (in fact I know I'm not because I have had this conversation with a number of people) who has cried apparently for no reason when in a crowd, where the crowd, en masse, expresses its emotion. This has happened to me on protest marches, at rugby matches and in church, as well as in the theatre and at music festivals. Leaving aside the idea that some of those venues had encouraged a bit of partying, I was interested to explore the idea of emotional contagion.

Primitive emotional contagion is defined as: 'The tendency to automatically mimic and synchronize expressions, vocalizations, postures, and movements with those of another person's and, consequently, to converge emotionally' (Hatfield et al. 1993). The concept, easily understandable, is that we are wired to pick up the smallest facial and verbal cues from another in order to know how to respond. Because the brain makes sense of all of this information, specifically in the amygdala, the brain's early warning system, it is common that we can find ourselves standing in others' shoes quite quickly. (This is quick because the amygdala is the part of the brain that is always on the look-out for threat, reacting to it in about 30 milliseconds – we react around 240 milliseconds later). In personality terms, empathy, however, is a slightly moveable feast – some find it easier than others to stand in the shoes of those they are with and be what we call empathetic.

All things being equal, however, emotional contagion explains why, quite quickly, emotion can be passed from one team member to another and without clear direction can affect the mood of the whole group.

There is an important note here for the leader – and that is that their mood has a disproportionate effect on the mood of their team. 'When leaders were in a positive mood, in comparison to a negative mood, (a) individual group members experienced more positive and less negative mood, and (b) groups had a more positive and a less negative affective tone' (Sy et al. 2005). The leader, therefore, has a huge influence on the mood of those around them. This is sometimes known as the 'shadow of the leader'. Being aware of that and managing that accordingly could be important.

What is the role of the coach and leader?

Given that team dynamics – the theories – stems from the psychological body of knowledge called psychodynamics, there is a basic assumption that, as described above, there is a conscious set of actions and behaviours that the team is engaged in – be it enjoyable or less enjoyable, and that those actions and behaviours are driven by subconscious forces. The more the team can be aware of what is driving their behaviour, and surface those subconscious forces, for themselves individually, or at times collectively, the more they will be able to engage in healthy conflict, build trust, feel safer to speak up, and engage in fruitful problem-solving and coordinated action, and as a result improve performance over time.

The constant question in the minds of the coach and the leader is what is being expressed but not articulated? What do the behaviours tell us about how people are thinking and feeling? What do those behaviours tell us about the relationships between team members? How is all of this enabling their work together or impairing it?

In *Reading the Room*, David Kantor (2012) describes four different positions team members can assume. These positions are:

- Movers who contribute their ideas and observations.
- Opposers who challenge those ideas and encourage exploration and movement.
- Followers who add to and develop those ideas and progress the conversations.
- Bystanders who observe, perhaps join the conversation later in a quieter way offer their different perspectives and support.

An observation grid can be created if that is helpful, checking behaviour against team members to assist the feedback process and notice the dynamic of the conversation and the team.

These roles are interchangeable though it's very useful to see, depending on the topic and the state of the team, who plays which role. It is useful for the team to experiment with changing roles – to be a bystander throughout may mean that the team is not getting the best from an individual. We have found this a useful and simple way of the team experiencing the group dynamic directly and examining how it impacts upon their work together.

Vignette: There is sometimes an individual team member who is an 'opposer' and who appears stuck in this position. We experienced one such occasion in a team in a high-stakes business and at a time when the team was newly formed. Having the four positions in mind helped us observe not just her contribution as an opposer but also the reaction of others and the positions they took. Over time, her position shifted to becoming a mover and follower. She had been caught, I think, by the anxiety of not being fully in control of the outcome and being with team members with whom she did not know well.

Team simulation

Given that team dynamics are not immediately 'visible' to the team, a device to bring them to the surface is important. What is sometimes very helpful is to invite the team to engage in a brief activity, seemingly unrelated to their work as a team. It is not sufficient for the coach to be able to observe the team dynamic, and sometimes it is not sufficient for team members to have it pointed out to them either. Sometimes, awareness can be developed more quickly by inviting the team to engage in action that simulates their work together. Examples include building the tallest spaghetti towers, creating bridges from lollipop sticks and asking the team to move an item from one place to another within set rules. There are lots of these different team exercises about.

Whatever exercises are selected, the most useful purpose to focus on is driving out the team dynamic. The outcome is team members being clear about the roles that they take up, their response to task and time pressure, their relationship with hierarchy and power, when and in what manner they engage with their colleagues, and for all of that what might be helping and hindering the team from moving forward.

What is critical is that there is a debrief that is meaningful following the activity. And that debrief then goes on to connect directly to the work the team is seeking to do together, and ideally the team is enabled to make some choices about how it operates in the future that can be enshrined in future agreements for which they hold each other accountable.

Here are some questions that might help that debrief:

- How successful was the team in completing the task?
- What process did you use?

- What roles did you each play?
- What qualities helped you in fulfilling the task?
- How might you change your approach if you did it again?
- What did you learn about the team and yourself?
- How satisfied were you with your contribution?

Vignette: A leadership team of six were building their understanding of the habits and patterns when alongside 10 other colleagues in the business. Together they constituted the leadership group. To take the lid off these habits and practices – the dynamic of the whole group – we invited them to divide into two mixed groups and compete to build the best bridge out of lollipop sticks. Creativity and colourful presentation would get extra points. This seemingly childlike game allowed everyone to experience directly the habits and patterns of the group. Both habits and patterns in the exercise matched their experience of each other at work. Exchange of feedback between the two parts of the group as well as to each other, one-on-one, was a powerful experience, which enabled the group to build more effective working relationships with which they could lead the business.

Assumptions

What is an assumption?

An assumption is something that we believe to be true but as yet cannot prove. By contrast, a belief is something that we 'know' to be true. We hold onto beliefs more tightly than assumptions, though assumptions can harden into beliefs rapidly.

Here is an example for you. Some of you will be old enough to remember the *Guardian* TV ad from the 1970s. It pictures a skinhead running along a pavement towards a man with a briefcase. One may assume that the skinhead is just about to steal the man's briefcase – he is running fast, and the man looks frightened when he sees the skinhead. What happens next, however, is that the skinhead pushes the man into the road and falls on top of him. The camera pans back to reveal a pile of bricks, that had been hanging over the man when he was on the pavement, crashing down just where the man had been. It missed the man by inches. The skinhead did, in fact, save the man's life. The strapline for the ad is 'get the full story', a powerful 30-second reminder of how much we can be held back by our own assumptions and how useful it is to have those assumptions challenged – in this case by reading a good newspaper. There is also a bit of social psychology here too – we are constantly in the process of constructing assumptions and therefore our reality with those around us – so understanding different perspectives, uncovering different assumptions that can be made, opens us up to seeing opportunities and resolving challenges more effectively and creatively.

How do we form assumptions?

We create assumptions to help us live in the world. In any situation we need to be able to interpret what is happening and be able to respond. We will never have all the 'facts', all the data, all the opinions from which to make decisions. Not only that, even if we have the same amount of data as others, we each may come back with different decisions, different ways of responding and acting. We create assumptions to quicken decision-making. It is automatic and we are largely unaware of it. At a basic level, we are faced with a situation, we interpret it and draw conclusions that guide our response.

It we look more closely at the process of interpretation we shall see that the 'data' flows through a series of filters. These filters are deployed in the moment to help us – some are deeply rooted and come from our upbringing, our experiences, our relationships, previous jobs and our professional training; some are developed more swiftly to deal with a situation. All assumptions, however, are formed to assist us to respond, take action, to direct our attention to what is important to us.

The Ladder of Inference (Argyris in Senge et al. 1994) maps out the process of assumption formation into discrete steps. The proposition is that we observe an occurrence and, depending on our physical position perhaps (as in the *Guardian* ad) as well as our upbringing, cultural filters and the like, we select some but not all of the data, and give those bits of data meaning. We then make assumptions about what happened and maybe even why it happened. We can then draw conclusions and form broader beliefs that move us to action. We can, of course, go 'up the ladder' extremely quickly. We are unaware of this process, largely. Each step, however, is fraught with difficulty – it's a wobbly ladder – and it is personal to us. We have our own filters, ways of selecting data and assumptions, and beliefs that already exist within us that are seeking confirmation. Before you know it, we are acting in a way that others may find surprising or unhelpful, despite our intention to the contrary.

Figure 10.1 The Ladder of Inference (Chris Argyris in Senge et al. 1994) adapted by David Webster

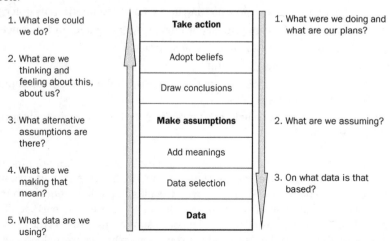

Why are assumptions important in a team?

Assumptions in a team are significant for the same reason that assumptions for an individual are important – and indeed organizations too. They drive us to action, even if the consequences turn out not to be what we like or intend. Simply adjusting the actions over time will not cut it – a more fundamental learning process needs to be deployed and assumptions challenged. The second reason that assumptions in the team is a useful area of focus is that they are much more malleable than beliefs or values. It is much easier to adjust assumptions, and it's much easier to hear them being articulated just beneath the surface in conversations that one might encounter in a team.

We have these key propositions. Assumptions in teams (and elsewhere) are:

- Neither right nor wrong
- More or less helpful to us
- Informing and in some cases driving our behaviour
- Thoughts it is useful to be curious about
- Thoughts that are useful to be held 'lightly'
- Thoughts that can be changed if they are less helpful to us
- Easy to spot if one listens for them
- Useful to inquire into such that they can be challenged if appropriate.

Uncovering basic assumptions

In coaching a team, we often introduce the idea of assumptions and explore others' understanding, experiences and awareness, uncovering some of their personal assumptions and when they have been challenged or changed. Another approach we use is simply to listen to them emerge from the conversation. This is especially helpful when, unanticipated, the team appears stuck in their conversation and bound by less helpful assumptions they are unaware of. Here is that process:

1 Observe the team in discussion, picking up as many assumptions as you can.
2 Introduce the idea of assumptions, perhaps using the Ladder of Inference.
3 Invite the team to share assumptions they notice they hold.
4 Share the ones you noted if helpful.
5 Invite the team to examine the consequences of holding each assumption and how helpful the assumption is.
6 What, therefore, are more helpful assumptions to hold and what might that enable the team to do?

Vignette: We worked with the leadership team of an organization bringing different partners together to serve the client. Within the conversation, which was focused on the challenges of engaging with the client at a time of great change for all parties, a number of assumptions began to rise to the surface. This unplanned occurrence allowed us to jot those assumptions down as the conversation unfolded – at first, the team didn't even notice what we were doing. Once the conversation drew to a close, we shared our notes – some were verbatim quotes, and some were implied assumptions that form the fabric of their discussion. We were then able to engage in a process that we had used many times, which was to examine how useful the assumptions were and whether the consequences of holding these assumptions were consequences they could live with. One of the assumptions, for instance, was 'in partnerships you have to avoid being too challenging'; another was 'poor performance can be tolerated'. Both of these assumptions were felt to be unintended consequences of the organizational culture that had been allowed to develop. They set about identifying manifestations of both these assumptions and agreeing how to counter them.

Trust

What is trust?

Our definition of trust is that it is a belief, present in a relationship, that another is:

- **Dependable:** That they will keep promises
- **Competent:** That they have the skill and experience required
- **Discrete:** That they will not betray confidences
- **Caring:** That they genuinely care for you and your interests.

This is based on the fact that most operational definitions examine trust as a belief about whether a partner is dependable (e.g. McAllister 1995), cares for your interests (e.g. Cook and Wall 1980), is competent (e.g. Mishra in Kramer and Tyler 1996), and/or will act with integrity (e.g. Robinson 1996).

Figure 10.2 The Trust Triangle (David Webster & Centre for Teams 2020)

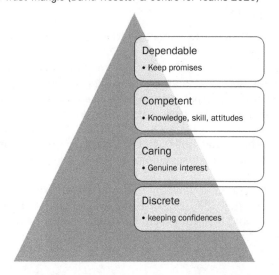

An example: my recent visit to Accident & Emergency (A&E)

I was recently treated by a doctor for a broken nose, which I sustained in a Tae Kwon Do sparring session. Let's look at the doctor who treated me, and how she built trust with me, which enabled her to do her job.

- **Dependability:** I arrive in A&E (or the ER if reading this in the US) with the broken nose. I am seen by the doctor. The break means that I need specialist attention, and the doctor says that she will need to check on a consultant's availability to perform a procedure. She returns five minutes later with details of where to go and who to ask for. She has won on dependability – not only was she a doctor in A&E who could diagnose the condition, and not only did she return, but she came back with specific instructions as she said she would.
- **Competence:** The doctor displays medical competence: she diagnoses my condition quickly by herself and, importantly, says that she was unable to perform the important procedure but that it was necessary; she also said, 'you need it done within the next few hours'. I do not yet trust her to perform quadruple bypass surgery on me, but I absolutely trust her judgement on my nose.
- **Discretion:** As she works, she asks about my family, my interest in sparring, about my work as a psychologist and why I like it. In turn, I ask similar questions of her. The more I share, the more I feel comfortable with her prodding and talking. I share because she asks questions in a way that makes me feel I have choice in what I share. I feel confident that she will not gossip. The initial gap between us begins to close and, as a result, she can work; and I can get my diagnosis.
- **Care:** By her actions, she shows she genuinely does care – beyond just doing her job, and despite the pressures in such an environment.

What is mutual trust?

Mutual trust is defined as 'the intention to accept vulnerability based upon positive expectations of the intentions or behaviour of another' (Rousseau in Dirks 1999) and as 'the expectation that others' future actions will be favourable to one's interests, such that one is willing to be vulnerable to those actions' (Robinson 1996). Trust is often cited as a key characteristic of effective teams (Jarvenpaa and Leidner 1999). It allows the development of mutual accountability, discussed in Chapter 9 on 'action'. The exchange of 'sincere promises' (Katzenbach and Smith 1993) results in greater commitment in teams. Trust also engenders psychological safety, a key feature of high performance teams.

Vignette: It was noon on the first morning of our two days together. My colleague and I invited the executive team to consider the qualities and behaviours that would help their conversations be successful in their work together. The stakes were high – complex expectations from multiple stakeholders and tough delivery targets. In this workshop, there was an opportunity to 'clear the decks' and refocus. Here, they could 'slow down to speed up'. Running somewhat against accepted development wisdom, we had waited until later in the first morning to hold this conversation. Waiting helps the team start to understand the rules they need. Our experience is that even in the first two hours, they will have become much more aware of what they need from each other to feel sufficiently safe in order to talk and progress. So, as with other teams before, instead of 'going through the motions' the conversation moved to trust – what it meant to them, how you build it, whether it was present in their team. They were striking at the nub of what often causes teams to flounder – a lack of trust.

How might you build trust in a team and, therefore, how might you display trustworthiness?

Table 10.1   Building Trust (David Webster & Centre for Teams 2020)

Component	
Dependability	Describe in a clear way what you will do and when you will do it by. Be clear about what you will not do – this may be more difficult but just as important. Be realistic and ensure you can and do deliver – this displays beyond doubt that you can be trusted.
Competence	Share the skills and experiences you can bring and be honest about tasks you know or sense are beyond you at that time. Ask for help if you get stuck, even if you have made a commitment to deliver alone. This shows you care about the outcome, but also that you can be a bit vulnerable; this disclosure encourages others to do the same.
Discretion	Share a little about yourself that displays what and who you care about. Think about the purpose you have in your work, what is important to you about what you do. This uncovers your values and intentions. Share with your team members what you see as your role in the team and why it is important to you. Avoid gossip or being roped into disclosing information shared in confidence.
Care for your team colleagues	Proactively offer your support to your colleagues – and not just when you need something directly in return. This carries with it an intrinsic reward – it will make you feel better and others will appreciate it.

A final word on trust

Trust is something that is built over time, so patience is required if you are really keen on building lasting trust. Take the care that is needed, and your team will flourish.

Psychological safety

Trust also engenders psychological safety, a state that allows for the surfacing of errors and the discussion of learning (Edmondson 1996 in Kayes 2004) and is crucial to avoid disaster (Kayes 2004). Psychological safety is defined as 'a shared belief that the team is safe for interpersonal risk-taking' (Edmondson 2019) and one in which 'people are comfortable being themselves'.

Psychological safety is so important and central to a team's ability to function for a number of reasons:

- It contributes to team members speaking up when they don't know something or when something has gone wrong or indeed is about to go wrong.
- It encourages the team to learn from its mistakes and explore those mistakes with less judgement and the inappropriate application of sanction or punishment.
- It ensures the team feel safe to explore, challenge, question, contribute. This supports innovation as we have already seen.
- Raises the level of challenge, and thereby improves the use of human resource. Each organization has what Edmondson describes as implicit 'theories of voice'. These determine when it is safe and when it is not safe to speak up. By failing to challenge these implicit rules and not sharing ideas, thoughts, observations and their own intelligence, the organization is deprived of the potential that difference brings.
- It enhances the team's ability to learn about the task as well as patterns of behaviour that stop the team from performing.
- It contributes to discussions and decision-making being a team sport rather than occurring only away from the team environment.
- Ultimately, it also makes for a healthier climate in which individuals can secure their own health and well-being – if one feels fearful, or anxious, that will have a physical as well as a psychological effect over time from which physical and mental illness can result.

In addition, there are direct performance improvement benefits. Research by Edmondson and Bayer concluded that 'Teams with psychological safety had high performance – which included measures of return on assets, and executive ratings of company goal achievement'. A by-product of their research also showed that 'process innovation can be a good way to boost firm performance, but a psychologically safe environment helps investment pay off' (Edmondson 2019). It also raises engagement where 'disengaged employees lead to safety risks and to staff turnover' following a study in healthcare.

What can the leader do?

In her book *Teaming*, Edmondson (2012) describes the leadership behaviours for cultivating psychological safety. These include being open to team members speaking up, saying when they don't know something, tolerating some measure of failure and the demonstrable desire to learn from success and failure alike, and following through on transgression of standards and agreements especially of behaviours. In short, the leader needs to behave in a way conducive to openness and with humility.

As Edmondson (1999) puts it:

> The leader's contribution to a climate of psychological safety is important. If the leader is supportive, coaching orientated and has non-defensive responses to questions and challenges, members are likely to conclude that the team constitutes a safe environment. In contrast if team leaders act in an authoritarian or punitive way team members may be reluctant to engage in the interpersonal risk involved in learning behaviours such as discussing errors, as was the case in the study of hospital teams.

Google's Project Aristotle

Google: In 2012, Google embarked upon a project codenamed Project Aristotle. The focus was to study teams across Google deploying the people analytics division to determine why some teams succeeded and others failed. Julia Rozovsky led the project. In Google's Effective Teams Guide, it reads:

> Of the five key dynamics of effective teams that the researchers identified, psychological safety was by far the most important. The Google researchers found that individuals in teams with higher psychological safety are less likely to leave Google, they're more likely to harness the power of diverse ideas from their teammates, they bring in more revenue, and they're rated as effective twice as often by executives Re:work.withgoogle.com.

This is backed up by the research from the 2017 Gallup poll that found 'only three in 10 employees strongly agree with the statement that their opinions count at work'. Gallup calculated that by 'moving that ratio to 6 in 10 employees, organisations could realize a 27% reduction in turnover, a 40% reduction in safety incidents and a 12% increase in productivity' (Edmondson 2019).

What can the coach do (alongside the leader) to engender a climate of psychological safety?

- **Build trust:** Given that trust is an important precursor to psychological safety, the coach can seek to build trust and connection and rapport with each team member individually. In building trust between coach and team member, the same rules apply as between team members themselves. The more the coach can be relied upon to follow through agreements, early on to display their competence, retain confidences as promised, the more individual team members will trust them, and that includes the leader.

- **Build confidence:** In addition, given that confidence sows the seeds for a feeling of greater safety, the more the coach can instil confidence in the process as well as team members' ability to function effectively together, however challenging the context of their task, the better.

- **Support boundary creation:** Build useful boundaries. The coach can also do very simple things like helping the team agree ground rules, qualities that they will display, behavioural expectations, and support the team to adhere to those agreements or adjust them when necessary. This not only builds trust and self-confidence in the team but continues to ensure that the team understands that it is ultimately their role to regulate their own environment.

- **Support the leader:** The coach can also support the leader to display the kinds of behaviours that create a safer environment. This may involve a new and fresh set of agreements between the leader and the led – the hotseat process (see below) is a useful way of instilling this, though there needs to be sufficient safety for it to work well. This means that it is not the coach giving the leader feedback from their own experience, but the team giving the feedback to the leader directly. The leader also has the opportunity to give feedback to the team such that the new agreement feels equitable to both parties. In addition, early on in the process, as has been previously described, it is useful to ensure that the leader does understand how the team experiences them. So, gathering feedback to share with the leader before the process starts is useful.

- **Observe and give feedback:** The coach can also observe the team in action noting the patterns of behaviour that are helpful and less helpful, who is speaking up and who is staying quiet, and the effect of the leader on the team and vice versa – and then, of course, share that feedback in a timely way with the team.

Two useful exercises to assist the emergence of psychological safety

1. Hot seat process

Purpose: To reset the contract between the leader and the led.

Process:

- Request that each team member spend 10 minutes noting down what they really value about the leader that helps them do their jobs individually and collectively, and what they would have the leader change that would affect their ability to deliver individually and function effectively as a team.

- The leader departs the room for 30 minutes.
- After 10 minutes of individual reflection, team members have an opportunity to share their reflections and come up with five things that they value about the leader and five things that they would have the leader change, and discuss how they will share them with the leader on return.
- The leader returns and sits in the middle of a semicircle so that they can see each member of the team and engage directly with them.
- The team shares things they value as well as things they would like the leader to change. The leader has the opportunity to enquire and consolidate understanding. Once the team has shared, the leader then has the opportunity to respond, affirming requests where possible, or negotiating with the team what they wish from the team in exchange.
- Once new agreements are made, these are noted by both parties, and any adjustments to behavioural expectations in the team ground rules can be made.

Vignette: We worked with the project leadership team responsible for delivery of a major installation in the energy sector. The leader was highly experienced with a reputation for being tough and likeable. The combination of line and function reports within the team meant that some knew the team leader well and some less well. The leader's exacting style was on occasion misinterpreted by newcomers. To reset the relationship before the team embarked upon the next phase of the project, we invited the team to engage in the 'hotseat' process. This allowed not only the building of relationships between the leader and led in creating a common platform for all team members and a common agreement but allowed a good negotiation to occur in real time between the two parties.

2. The elk

While working in Norway, we discovered that what we know as elephants in the room are elks in Norway. They are the 'undiscussables', those subjects of conversation that are known to most, if not everyone, in the team, but not discussed. The very act of talking about them frees up a conversation about psychological safety and its importance, as well as clearing the elk from the room. These undiscussables, if they remain hidden, are always a drain on the team – both in relationships and in task delivery. It's the coach's role and the leader's to spot them or notice that they may be there and raise the question, promoting a healthier environment.

The idea of the elephant in the room in the UK is often understood well by teams. It usually takes some time for the team to feel that it is safe enough to share what they feel are the elephants. Sometimes, it is a team member who, in the middle of a process, voices the need to share what the elephants are. This is a good sign. A sign that psychological safety is being built. The elephants conversation serves to build greater psychological safety. And, in turn, it will build more trust and confidence in the team if those elephants are addressed.

Behavioural expectations

What are they?

'Behavioural expectations' is a more explicit phrase to describe ground rules for a team. They are quite literally a clear articulation of how team members are expected to behave in order to support the effective functioning of the team. In a sense, team members already know how to behave. 'Group norms' are not visible but are acquired by team members over time and dictate how they should or should not behave. They may well be a function of the wider organization and its culture.

Why are they helpful?

However, the surfacing of those group norms and harvesting behaviours that are already being exhibited and are helpful to the team and its work together we see as critical. This is for four reasons: first, a clear and tangible expression of behavioural expectations makes it easier for the team to establish its identity and team culture supportive of its objectives. Second, they provide a psychological boundary within which team members know that it is safe – it builds psychological safety. Third, it makes it easier to induct new team members, who can immediately see how they are expected to behave. Fourth, it gives the team an opportunity to build mutual accountability in execution of the tasks and building relationships with those beyond the team. If a team member varies from the expectations as agreed, they can, in turn, expect feedback and, ultimately, consequence from their peers.

We see many such agreements, and sadly many that are ignored, mostly we think because they have not been made at a point in the team's life when there is a felt need for them to exist and be upheld. Many books and eminent researchers will tell you that to make it safe for people to have a conversation you need some ground rules. This is true. However, so often is this call made and so many ground rules are collected that I think they become fairly meaningless. It's been our habit in the last few years to wait until, say, after lunch on the first day of a two-day workshop to ask the team how the conversations have been to that point and what kind of behaviours have helped the conversations be successful, when they have. And, conversely, if they have been less successful what would have helped. This makes the conversation entirely real, and highly productive. We are careful, however, to make specific requirements of the team, at a very simple level within the first few minutes of the workshop, so this second round comes very much from the team.

Often, these ground rules, or sets of behaviours, are adopted by the team to be used more broadly, and beyond the work we are doing with them. That's when we know they have worked. It is interesting also that many expectations set in this way are not really behaviours – they are qualities of a conversation that you may feel but cannot observe. You can observe, for instance, that everybody gives their positive consent to a decision, but you cannot observe honesty. So, ensuring that the behaviours, if that is what you're going for, are observable is important. Often, therefore, we ask for behaviours, and ground rules and some qualities. But even when qualities are tabled, we invite the team to be specific about how they would know that 'honesty', for instance, was being displayed. It's important that the team feel that the session ground rules are theirs rather than yours, as a coach. If you are a leader, then they also need to be owned by the team even if the leader has the final veto. This is setting a boundary – which makes it safer for people to speak up. Throughout a coach's work with the team, therefore, and indeed the leader's work with the team, it will be useful for the team to pause and reflect on whether the behaviours are being displayed, and if they are not, then what changes would they make to them in order for them to be useful again. And what behavioural changes does the team need to make in order that their decisions and conversations are of as high a quality as possible.

Leadership team in Leading Alliances plc

- Celebrate success
- Seek counsel and opinions of others
- Have the courage of your convictions
- Raise a flag to highlight good and bad
- Cascade positive behaviours
- See the positives and enjoy the journey
- Live the values (of the organization)
- See every challenge as an opportunity
- Avoid blame – resolve
- Challenge to make things better.

Belief and commitment

Team belief and commitment

Teams that believe they will be successful are more likely to be successful. That collective belief supports the creation of a team identity, greater unity and coherence. So, the team building belief in itself is important. Let's look at the concepts of commitment and belief in more detail:

Potency is 'the group's collective belief that it can be effective' and it 'significantly predict(s) group effectiveness' (Guzzo et al. 1993). There is 'a strong positive relation between potency and performance' – greater even than ability (Allen and Hecht 2004). The individual equivalent from which it is drawn is self-efficacy – 'an individual's appraisal of the likelihood of being able to carry out a task successfully' (Bandura 1989). The process of self-motivation is one of creation of disequilibrium (by setting challenging goals) and then working one's way towards them, overcoming obstacles along the way. In overcoming obstacles, one has an opportunity for 'mastery experiences' – a bringing together of learning with the task.

Commitment is very similar. Again, the research is pretty clear. The greater the commitment that the team has to the task, and working effectively on the task together, the more the team will be successful. This, of course, is closely related to the effort that team members are prepared to expend in helping the team be successful – the more effort, the more success, all other things being equal. Clearly, if the strategy that the team is pursuing is entirely wrong, then the effort won't help. And that goes back to the quality of the decision-making that, in turn, is affected by the quality of the dynamic between team members as well as, of course, the level of skill and experience each brings.

In summary, then, teams that can develop commitment to deliver and a belief that they will, are more likely to be successful (Allen and Hecht 2004).

All of these elements will play out (or not) in the team to some degree – and the coach and the leader can be open to observations that these are present in the team or absent. Ironically, the more 'coherent' the team is in its dynamic fed by commitment and belief (see Chapter 7 on 'Purpose'), the more it may be prey to a team dynamic 'trap' – over-compliance – or what is known as 'groupthink'.

Groupthink

Groupthink is defined by Janis (1972) as 'a mode of thinking that people engage in when they are deeply involved in a cohesive "in-group", when the members' strivings for unanimity override their motivation to realistically appraise alternative courses of action'. He goes on:

> the more amiability and esprit de corps among members of a policy-making in group, the greater is the danger that independent critical thinking will be replaced by groupthink . . . The social constraint consists of the members' strong wish to preserve the harmony of the group, which inclines them to avoid creating any discordant arguments or schisms.

A good example of this was the 1986 NASA *Challenger* disaster, which saw seven crew members die as the shuttle launched. The Presidential Commission's report highlights the 'groupthink' that stopped a more detailed examination of the risk of catastrophic failure in one part of the shuttle prior to launch. Below is a summary of that report.

Report of the Presidential Commission on the space shuttle *Challenger* disaster (Janis 1991)

Overestimation of the group. There was an 'illusion of invulnerability', which stemmed from the fact that 'the American space programme had never experienced an in-flight fatality'; and a belief in the inherent morality of the group – as one NASA engineer commented: 'I had the distinct feeling we were in the position of having to prove that it was unsafe instead of the other way around'.

Close-mindedness. Collective rationalization with a 'hear no evil, see no evil, speak no evil' mindset was consolidated with 'out-group stereotypes', which focused on NASA's view of contractors. For example, the contractor engineers implied they wished to delay the launch until the temperature of the fuel rose to 53°F. The NASA manager reportedly asked (sarcastically) whether the contractors expected NASA to wait 'until April' to launch the shuttle.

Pressures towards conformity Self-censorship came at critical moments. One such moment was contractor engineer George MacDonald wanting to postpone the flight. But instead of clearly stating 'I recommend we don't launch below 53°', he offered an equivocal opinion. He suggested that 'lower temperatures are in the direction of badness for both O-rings' (the component that proved to be the point of failure). What did he think they should do? From his tempered words it's hard to tell. Conformity was also created through:

- **The illusion of unanimity:** NASA managers perpetuated the fiction that everybody was fully in accord on the launch recommendation. They admitted to the Presidential Commission that they didn't report their colleagues 'on again-off again' hesitancy to their superiors. As often happens in such cases, the flight readiness review team interpreted silence as agreement.

- **Direct pressure on dissenters:** NASA managers were fearful of an American public who might regard them as inept if they did not launch. In addition, management was fearful of losing future NASA contracts.

- **Self-appointed 'mind guards':** Mind guards protect a leader from assault by troublesome ideas. NASA managers insulated Jesse Moore from the debate over the integrity of the rocket booster seals. Even though one of the contractor engineers was an expert on O-rings, he later bemoaned that he was 'not even asked to participate in giving input to the final decision charts'.

How do you avoid groupthink?

Given the magnitude of the example above, it's important to realize that it can happen at a more local level too. The consequences may or may not be as catastrophic, yet if you work in a high-risk environment or you are making significant decisions that affect others way beyond the team, it is best to be on the look-out. What can you do?

- Be aware that it happens and be open to the signals – lack of engagement from some, an easy solution that is not questioned, making assumptions that could lead to error.

- Play devil's advocate – or appoint someone in the team to do so – so that challenge can be built into the process.

- Gather more data and table data that is counter to the current wisdom.
- Plan well so that all the data can be scrutinized.
- Invite challenge from outside the team – other teams, other parts of the organization or an expert from beyond the organization.
- Ask questions of each other in the team, rooting out assumptions and beliefs so they can be challenged.
- Bring in the quietest team members into the discussion.
- Ensure you have all the risks out early and work to mitigate them as you work.
- Create a culture of psychological safety and trust.

Summary

- Team dynamics are the 'social forces and influences at play' in a team. The health of the team dynamic will make or break the team.
- A healthy team dynamic requires that the team develops sufficient trust, psychological safety, alignment on expected behaviours, commitment and belief, and supportive assumptions.
- Emotional contagion means that moods and emotions travel fast between team members.
- An assumption is something that is believed to be true but cannot as yet be proven. They can be helpful or unhelpful, so spotting them and adjusting those assumptions to align with desired outcomes is useful.
- Trust is a belief you hold that another is dependable, competent, discreet and caring. Building trust in a team is central to a healthy dynamic and effective action together. Trust can be built by supporting trustworthy behaviour between team members.
- Psychological safety in a team is 'a shared belief that the team is safe for interpersonal risk-taking' (Edmondson 1999). It is seen as one of the most critical influences on the health and effectiveness of the team. A coach and team leader can engender a climate of psychological safety by encouraging trust, confidence, boundary creation and by modelling behaviour.
- Behavioural expectations or how team members expect each other to behave. Alignment on behaviours is an important boundary for the team and supports a healthy dynamic and team effectiveness.
- Team belief and commitment are also important ingredients in a healthy team dynamic, although caution needs to be exercised to avoid groupthink as a function of a surplus group coherence, fed by commitment and belief (see Chapter 7 on 'Purpose').

11 Team leadership

The forgotten art

Team leadership is really the forgotten art. There is no more important role in any organization than those who lead small teams. Given the critical place that teams play in all our lives, learning how to lead them effectively is similarly critical. Without effective team leadership, the teams will falter, and the organization will fail its team members.

Here, we look at the role of the leader and propose six elements of the forgotten art of team leadership. At the end of the chapter, the leader can check themselves against a basic coaching skills questionnaire.

Team leadership: leading and transforming the team 'system'

Team leadership: is this a forgotten art?

If the 2008 crash taught us anything, it was that small groups of people can have a huge impact on others and that if there is no 'systems leadership' we can be in trouble. How small teams are led – be it the leadership team of a bank, an oil rig or a charity, or a project team in an ad agency – has a fundamental impact on its success and that of the enterprise as a whole. And yet, somehow, we don't attend to this art – has it been forgotten? One of the most famous examples of great team leadership is drawn from the Antarctic just over 100 years ago and Shackleton's leadership of a heroically unsuccessful team and their bid to make it to the South Pole. Their failure could be marked as a success in that nobody lost their lives despite the extraordinarily severe conditions. This is commonly attributed to Shackleton's leadership, and the individual commitment of team members to apply their ingenuity and skill and resilience to their situation. Yet this was a relatively small team of 20 rather than a whole enterprise.

The leader plays an invaluable part in good teamwork – shaping goals, motivating, supporting learning, providing the team with air cover – yet their very presence can threaten teamwork given they are 'in charge' of the team's efforts. This is sometimes called the 'team paradox' and one that we found often presents team leaders with a dilemma as to where to strike the balance on a number of spectrums – including task vs relationship focus and the right operational distance between them and the team.

While there are a thousand programmes to develop leadership, many deal with self-management and many more with progressing the organization's longer-term response to its environment – few focus on the way in which most of us experience our work – the small team. There are few conversations about how to be a great team member and fewer still on how those teams can effectively be led. Somehow, the art of small team leadership has been forgotten.

Work now is more complex than it was even 20 years ago – many are now members of several teams, 'matrixed', all with important briefs, making significant calls on team members' time and capacity; and members of the same team are now likely not to be in the same location for at least some of their work. Ensuring success despite these shifts is now the game.

The team leader's role

A team leader – be that the managing director or project lead – is instrumental in team success. The team leader's role comprises three different parts (Downey 2003), each of which has a different intention relating to the team's performance – either because it's directly related to clarity of task and expectation, or indirectly because it is about how the team thinks and feels and how it translates those thoughts and feelings into action.

The three different parts of the leader's role are as follows:

- **Leading:** The purpose of leading is to clarify direction. Often, this is the long-term direction of the team and its mission or vision. Within this clarity of direction comes inspiration, influence, some guiding, and also showing the ability to be influenced by the team and its ideas and intelligence.
- **Managing:** The purpose of managing is to ensure compliance for agreements and commitments made. Here the leader is holding the team to account for commitments made and ensuring it follows through on those commitments. They keep the focus on delivery as well as managing the expectations of wider stakeholders. Here the leader focuses on their ability to control events.
- **Coaching:** The purpose of coaching is to challenge and support team members and the team as a whole to learn and perform to their best within their commitments. Here the leader is encouraging learning from each other as well as learning bought in from outside to help resolve conflict, create new ideas and innovative solutions, support the team to solve its own challenges and questions, and help the team continue to grow both as people and as a unit of performance. Indeed, 'the ability of a team leader to help the team and team members become more capable is intrinsic to the team's growth and its performance, alongside performing management and leadership tasks that give the team direction and space' (Hackman 2002).

Crucial to all of these are the **relationships** the leader builds both within and beyond the team; without these they will not be able to build the team and enable it to achieve its goals. They are the foundation of success and without them the team leader and the team do not stand a good chance of succeeding.

Figure 11.1 The Leader's Role (based on Downey 2003)

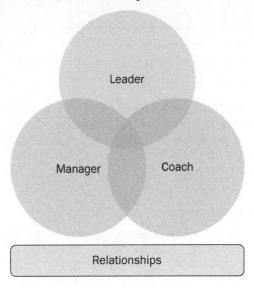

Many times, we have shared this idea of team leadership with leaders by starting by asking them what key activities they are engaged in. Without sharing the model itself, we map their responses to where the model will eventually sit. It may not come as a surprise that the majority of activity sits in the managing circle. Some sit in leading and occasionally there is some coaching going on. Usually, that coaching occurs one-on-one rather than of the team. This very unscientific poll might indicate that organizations are still primarily focused on compliance and task rather than creating the conditions for growth and excellence. What is crucial to understand though is that on the left-hand side the organization still, rightfully, retains authority – it has the right to decide where the organization is going on what it does day-to-day. And at a team level that is broadly still true – the leader still has the authority to make decisions, change the structure, change roles, hire and fire. Yet on the right-hand side, the team and its team members have authority. That is true even if it is not acknowledged or attended to by the team leader. Therefore, if the team leader does not ensure genuine enrolment, alignment and a healthy team dynamic, team members will vote with their feet, with a lack of discretionary effort.

Team coaching is an act of leadership

This book is aimed both at would-be or current practitioners of the team coaching art, as well as the teams and leaders they work with. But it's worth mentioning that for a leader – indeed for an external coach too – Hackman and Wageman (2005) proposed that there were three different kinds of coaching available; all are 'acts of leadership':

- Educational, which focuses on the development of skill of team members and the team as a whole
- Motivational, which intends to develop the effort, energy, motivation, commitment and belief of team members
- Strategic, which aims to integrate the team in order that it can be effective together.

All of these are available to the leader, and this reinforces the broad point that I hope we make throughout this book that whichever is selected the coach and leader are clear on the intention they have in engaging with the team. The clearer that intention, the easier it will be to see whether it will work, and what is required to make it work well.

What the research can tell us

There is a surprising paucity of research that deals specifically with a small team leadership as distinct from leadership of individuals or of whole enterprises. De Church et al. (2010) in Salas et al. (2005) reviewed the body of leadership literature from 1985 to 2009 and showed that only 11 per cent of leadership studies focused on the team level of analysis. There is clearly a gap here.

The leader's positive expectations of success contribute to team potency (meaning belief) and performance (Eden 1985). To the author's knowledge, there is no current research on the congruence between **the leader's journey** and the team's journey, though congruence appeared to be helpful in the teams we have worked with and experienced, with successful leaders we have known expressing personal learning as a result of their leadership. In addition, the **leader encouraging learning** in the team is crucial – 'teams that function with multiple goals require greater learning in order to adapt to changing organisational circumstance' (Kayes 2004). Hackman (1990) sees the leader encouraging the whole team to deal with difficult problems together as a pre-requisite for high performance.

Leadership effectiveness is indicated by, broadly, 'success in mobilizing and motivating followers to contribute to the achievement of collective objectives' (Yukl 2002). Indicators of leadership effectiveness at a team level include psychological states such as collective efficacy (meaning confidence), team processes such as cooperation, and behaviours such as team performance, creativity and decision-making quality (Van Knippenburg in Salas et al. 2005). There is an emerging body of knowledge on empowering leadership behaviour, which to varying degrees has consistently contributed to team synergy. This is not a great surprise given that team empowerment is about 'giving responsibility to the team and encouraging team members to use this responsibility and conveying a sense of trust in the team' (Stewart 2006). In a sense, empowering the team necessarily requires the team to work together rather than be reliant on the leader for making it happen. Meta-analytic evidence speaks to the effectiveness of team leadership. Wang et al. (2014) show that overall 'shared leadership' where 'all team members at least to a certain extent share in fulfilling the leadership role – guiding and leading each other', is positively related to team effectiveness. So the emerging research, although not substantial in volume, indicates reasonably clearly, with some caveats, that small teams benefit from leaders who share power with the team or indeed share their leadership of the team.

Top management teams

Many top teams, who run a whole enterprise (and some we have found in part enterprise) operate like a gathering of independent sovereign nations, rarely collaborating and focusing exclusively on their own part of the map to the exclusion of the whole. If this is your top team and you are the CEO, then here are ways to encourage greater collaboration and real teamwork, which chime well with the Adaptable Team Framework:

- **Team identity:** Should be clear and felt by the team and can be aided by creating a vision, and being clear on its purpose as a team and agreeing behavioural expectations.
- **Teamwork:** The team should engage in real work together, including joint problem-solving sessions.
- **The composition of roles:** Giving executives pan-business initiatives to conduct on behalf of the team, and hiring team members who have multidisciplinary experience.
- **Team incentives:** They should be geared not just to individual reward but team reward.
- **The CEO as role model:** As the team leader there is a powerful opportunity to demonstrate the behaviours that are going to encourage participation. These include being open, encouraging personal and business agendas to be shared, discussing agreements that can be made away from the team, ensuring minority views are heard, and that disagreements can be had without recrimination.

Shadow of the leader

One piece of research I have found consistently useful is the role of the mood of the leader in the team's work together and, by implication, its chances of success. Mood is different from emotion. Emotions are experienced as a result of a particular incident or occurrence. Moods are generalized feelings. Sy et al. (2005) concluded from their experimental research that:

> when leaders were in a positive mood, in comparison to a negative mood, (a) individual group members experienced more positive and less negative mood, and (b) groups had a more positive and a less negative affective tone. The authors also found that groups with leaders in a positive mood exhibited more coordination and expended less effort than did groups with leaders in a negative mood.

It is easy to see how mood can affect others, and the leader's positional authority and power can be seen as a way of controlling the team – even if this is subconscious on the leader's part. We have all 'walked on eggshells' while the 'bad mood' of the leader was 'worked around'; or been 'afraid to ask' when the leader seems upset and work slows to accommodate their different pace. Paying attention to this is instructive for the leader. That is not to say the leader does not need to show emotion and vulnerability at times – this can encourage a level of honesty in the team that is productive. However, if the leader is not providing sufficient energy and direction to the team, the team will falter. Uncertainty (which is what poor mood management of a leader brings) breeds an anxiety that is toxic to teams – sooner or later this becomes an 'elephant in the room', something that the team members avoid talking about in the team. The next question is what else is the team not talking about?

Example of the effect of leader mood: Years ago, I coached two members of the top team of a regulator, one of whom was the leader. His personality was stamped firmly on the whole organization and he had a very particular way of doing things, being highly controlled in his approach. When I attended one or two of the top team meetings, the behaviour of the team mirrored the leader, and they were slightly fearful of deviation and testing things out.

Bringing back the art: the top six for the small team leader artist

I wouldn't disagree with anything shared for CEOs above, though more broadly, here is a small contribution to the gap in thinking on team leadership – an aide memoire for the leader seeking to get the best of their team – be it a senior leadership team or a project team, short term or long term, virtual or real.

1 **Where are we really going?** In these days of empowerment and employee engagement, it is easy to forget that what is most sought is clarity of direction – where are we going? Whether this is created by a comprehensive programme of team conversations or whether it is declared and understanding deepened through discussion matters much less than the end game – it must be clear, understood and accepted by team members.

2 **Job descriptions are irrelevant – what do you really need from each other to deliver?** Roles, particularly at a senior level, are always negotiated though we act as though they are not and avoid the negotiations that are required for expectations to be clear. Be honest, when was the last time you looked at your job description? Much more important are the conversations in the team: between the leader and the team and between team members. At a simple level, these need to cover, for each person, their objectives, their requests and their offers. And the rooky's error is to leave it there – as a leader you need to model and encourage a continuous exchange of good

quality feedback to ensure that mission-critical relationships (where the currency is trust) are constantly improving.

3 **Does the team have a map?** It's very useful for the team to know early on in the team's life that there are some fundamentals to get right both in the task and its clarity as well as in the relationships they need to establish. If these are not attended to, that lack of clarity and understanding of each other will create anxiety, which will come out when you least expect it. I bet you have a plan for the delivery of Y project by X date (if you don't, you probably need that) but do you have a roadmap for the team's journey? Do you have a clear picture, which is truly embraced by the team, of it working at its peak and a deeply felt understanding of what that journey will be like? Have you ever taken a step back at a meeting that is going southwards and discussed if this difficulty is normal at this stage in the life of a team? If you do, solutions are easier to find, tasks easier to complete and differences between people easier to use for effective decision-making.

4 **How safe do you make it?** We shall talk more about psychological safety when we come to the chapter on team dynamic, but suffice it to say that the leader plays a hugely important part in making the conversations that occur in the team 'safe'. By this I mean that team members are sufficiently assured that should they raise questions, make observations, disclose opinions or, indeed, share of their more personal side, they will not be met with embarrassment, ridicule or shame. This may seem a small issue in the modern workplace; however, in the drive for performance and the desire for many leaders to progress in their careers, these things can be overlooked, and their importance underplayed. However senior, if you do not feel that your contribution is taken seriously and respected you will play safe and minimize your contribution. The team leader plays an important part in encouraging safety, mainly by demonstrating that it is safe and modelling both the sharing of opinion, as well as the asking of questions in a 'safe' manner.

5 **Slow down to speed up.** When was the last time your team meeting contained the question 'what do we need to learn as a team that will help us succeed?'? This question appears to be more acceptable to ask individuals (in the annual appraisal probably, though less at other times . . .). We are always learning, all the time – we do stuff, reflect on it, we make connections and decide how to respond. Mostly, we don't talk about it and it happens automatically – and most teams are caught in the doing stuff and making decisions part of the cycle. Without reflecting and making connections between things, we fail to come to real shared views or genuinely common goals, and we fail to understand how we can be really effective in our work together – and the result? Poor decisions, half-baked activity, the poor use of team member capability and, at its worst, sabotaged team effort as frustration rises and comes out in peculiar places.

6 **Engage with the world and help your colleagues do the same.** All teams desire to have influence in their context, and indeed a team only exists in context – what is in that context that will help the team or challenge the

team? How clear are the needs of senior management? Your internal and external clients and customers? Your staff? These are all stakeholder groups and your ability to understand and manage relationships with them and learn from them is crucial. The best way to start doing this is to develop a stakeholder plan and have it be part of the regular conversations with the team.

So, there we have it – not only the top six but a pretty good start in championing the art of small team leadership.

Check your coaching skills

Check your coaching skills as a leader

We worked with 'Oil & Gas plc' in the Far East a little while ago. They had sought to create a coaching and performance culture to engender swifter and higher quality problem-solving in their geographically separated parts, more responsibility further down in the business, greater learning, and a continuous improvement drive. As part of our work with them we devised a simple assessment process to benchmark leaders' current ability as coaches and engender a focus on a shift in conversation. It is a 360° instrument, which also had the benefit of enrolling their teams in their development. We share the questionnaire here to assist leaders in assessing their own coaching capability at a very simple level, remembering, of course, that coaching sits alongside the ability to manage and lead as well. Leaders can score themselves out of 10 and give themselves a mark out of 220 and then a percentage score. Where can you focus, therefore?

The Oil & Gas plc coaching skills questionnaire

Coaching involves facilitating a conversation to accelerate the performance and development of others. This is seen as instrumental in being able to Innovate, Accelerate and Learn, which is core to the Oil & Gas plc way and to the future growth of the business. As the organization develops its skill in this area, it is useful for leaders to gain insight into how others experience them as they enhance their coaching capability.

This questionnaire is about your colleague, Leader X, and their use of coaching or a coaching approach in their leadership style, in interactions with you.

Leader X has invited you to share your observations to help them learn. Your responses will be confidential and anonymous. This will take you no longer than 8 minutes.

Listens to understand

This leader . . .

• Is genuinely interested to hear my ideas for improving the business

- Listens to me without interrupting
- Understands my perspective when I share it
- Uses good questions and listening even when under operational pressure.

Utilizes the most appropriate coaching approach

This leader . . .

- Adjusts their approach depending on the kind of conversation I need
- Avoids doing my thinking for me
- Does not inappropriately default to 'telling' people what to do when the operational pressure is rising.

Builds trust

This leader . . .

- Creates an environment where I feel I can talk openly
- Helps establish mutual expectations for our work together.

Speaks with intent

This leader . . .

- Brings focus to our conversations
- Brings clarity of outcome to our conversations
- Does not waffle.

Asks powerful questions

This leader . . .

- Asks questions that challenge my thinking
- Asks questions that help me create solutions for myself
- Asks questions to help me understand what I can improve
- Is genuinely interested in my response to questions.

Provides feedback and feedforward

This leader . . .

- Gives frequent feedback based on their direct observations
- Balances positive feedback with developmental feedback
- Gives feedback which I find useful.

Understands the context

This leader . . .

- Raises my awareness of the impact my actions have on other people
- Shares their knowledge of the business context to support my learning and our conversations
- Coaches when it is most helpful to do so.

Please share one observation for each of the following questions:

- What does Leader X do to help you learn and perform to your best?
- What would you have Leader X do that would be even more helpful?

Summary

- There are three elements of a leader's role: leading, managing and coaching.
- Within the leader's role, team coaching is an act of leadership.
- There is a paucity of research on small team leadership, though the effect leaders can have on the ability of the team to function effectively is profound.
- The top six prompts for a small team leader are:
  - Where are we going?
  - What do you really need from each other to deliver?
  - Do you have a map?
  - How safe do you make it?
  - Slow down to speed up
  - Engage with the world and help your colleagues do the same
- Check your coaching skills as a leader and continue to develop that capacity.

12 Team learning rhythm
Sustaining team performance

Learning how to learn

We are learning all the time. Elevating learning to a conscious level in a team ensures that the team is actively learning from its experience and can immediately make adjustments to what it is doing, the way that it is doing it, and how it can continue to influence others and deliver results. Here we examine three levels of team learning and a rhythm of team learning that will ensure high and sustainable team performance.

Team learning

The ability of the team to learn is central to its ability to sustain performance over time. The old adage 'madness is to keep on doing the same things and expecting a different result' is perhaps useful to bear in mind here. Although tried and tested mechanisms of applying knowledge in a technical sense are, of course, central to a professional role, all businesses function effectively or not as a result of the interface between the technical and the social, the rational and the emotional.

Team learning 'is the process of aligning and developing the capacity of its team members to create the results its members truly desire' (Senge et al. 1994). In a broader sense, it is best seen as 'a process and attempt to articulate the behaviours through which outcomes such as adaptation to change, greater understanding, or improved performance in teams can be achieved' and the testing of assumptions and discussion of different opinions in the team (Edmondson 1999).

Team learning, therefore, can focus not just on improving the knowledge and action learning cycle but going deeper and understanding the drivers for application of that knowledge in a more or less effective way both at an individual as well as a team level. A leadership team or a project team has within it, as has been discussed earlier, a dynamic all of its own. Understanding and continuing to improve that dynamic has a material effect on the quality of the actions and understanding where those thoughts and feelings come from and ensuring that they are aligned with the outcomes that you wish is crucial.

What if you don't have team learning embedded?

The 1996 Everest disaster

In 1996 Mount Everest experienced its biggest climbing disaster to date with 15 people dying that year – eight from three expeditions. What happened has been the subject of both academic study and books, one written by a member of one of the expeditions, John Krakauer. The tragedy revealed both the flawed heroism and perhaps hubris of Rob Hall, one of the leaders of the expedition, who sadly lost his life that year, as well as the inability of the team to learn as events unfolded. There was a huge amount of experience contained in the leadership of the expeditions involved, and that experience involves knowing about important routines and climbing ground rules. One of them for Everest is that irrespective of whether you have summited, you turn back after a certain time has passed, otherwise on the way down it will get dark and the weather will turn. The team leaders struck agreements between them as to how they would manage their respective teams when seeking to summit. All was set.

So, what happened?

At the core of events was the inability of the expedition teams to adapt to changes in weather, the health of team members and situations they were faced with on the hill. As Kayes (2004, 1263) comments, 'Unless a team does learn collectively, it will not be able to strategize effectively or maintain potency' (belief that it will be successful). They made assumptions that were incorrect but had no way of either challenging those assumptions or fixing problems when the teams set off. Summit fever took over, and the expedition leader and one of his party did not turn back at the appointed time and remained stuck on the hill when bad weather struck. Fixed ropes that were assumed to be present at the base of the Hillary Step, very close to the summit, had worn away and there was no plan for fixing them. The two members of the expedition who arrived finding no ropes, waited in the cold. As the weather turned, expedition members became strung over a large distance and the over-reliance on close leadership and supervision began to tell. Once it became clear that everybody needed to get off the hill, it was already too late for some and for others it was a long cold night from which frostbite and snow blindness would result.

The three levels of team learning

It is important to distinguish different kinds of learning in teams in order to ensure that the right conversations are being had to be able to generate a different and better result. There are three different kinds of learning, which we describe as 'levels of learning', both for a team as well as an individual.

Level 1: Action and results. Level 1 learning is the most transactional and simple level of learning and the one that we engage in perhaps most frequently. We may see learning as the acquisition of knowledge and then the ability to apply that knowledge, improving our ability to apply that knowledge over time. In the team, team members may engage in more or less coordinated action aimed to produce a result. Depending on how it goes, the team may then review the outcome and decide what they need to change in their actions in order to be able to adjust the result. An example may be an executive team presenting to a board. The presentation does not go according to plan and in review the team decides to spend more time on preparation next time and have a run-through.

Level 2: Dynamics and action. Level 2 learning (dynamic learning) strikes at a deeper level. It is about seeing a situation, opportunity, problem or dilemma differently. Using the language used earlier, we may adjust our assumptions about that situation, we may challenge our self-doubt and build our belief in success by looking at what is working and what has been achieved, we may express how we feel about the situation and in doing so be able to feel differently about the next round of action. Going back to our example, we may see the board presentations differently. What if we saw them as an opportunity to build relationships, or gain agreement for specific decisions we are taking, or a way of enlisting specific support in resolving wicked problems? This starts to change the way that we experience those meetings as well as how we might prepare.

Level 3: Purpose and dynamics. Level 3 learning is deeper still. It strikes at how we see our purpose and why the team exists. It is about how we experience ourselves as a team and therefore our identity as a team. This is the most transformative level and is the most fundamental. Again, going back to our example of the executive board presentation, we may return to conversations about our purpose. This may uncover or reconfirm why we exist and therefore how to go about dispatching our purpose in a different way. When we show up at the board the next time displaying our purpose, which we've decided is 'to lead the business', including the board, it is likely that we will 'show up' in a very different way, displaying different levels of confidence and belief in our ability. The quality of the conversation is raised. A better result is possible.

The team needs to be open to all of these levels at different points in time and be able to develop a curiosity as to which level needs to shift in order that more of the team's potential to perform becomes available to them.

Question for a team: At what level do you need to learn at present to be able to produce and sustain results?

Team learning rhythm

Most teams establish an operational rhythm – a series of meetings with which the team monitors its progress and plans for action. To ensure that the team continues to learn from its experiences, it is also useful to establish a learning rhythm, with regular and effective conversations that not only monitor progress in a meaningful way but also slow the team down long enough for it to learn about how to deliver a better and more sustainable outcome. The coach can assist the team in establishing its own learning rhythm at those three different levels – actions, dynamics and purpose. This then becomes fundamental to the team's ability to adapt to changing circumstances and requirements.

Figure 12.1 The Adaptable Team: The Three Levels of Learning
Graphic by Red Giant, London

LEVEL 1

RESULTS ACTION

The team adjusts the actions it takes to get results by looking at new data or acquiring new ideas, skills or knowledge. **This leads to an incremental improvement in results.**

LEVEL 2

ACTION DYNAMICS

Team members shift the way they think and feel about themselves, the task or each other; they use different perspectives and challenge assumptions. **This leads to a step change in results.**

LEVEL 3

DYNAMICS PURPOSE

The team examines its purpose and identity in context, and in relation to the stakeholders and systems it serves. **This is the foundation for high and sustainable results.**

There is another reason that rhythm is important. Organizational life has a rhythm as described. Our lives have rhythm too – the seasons, academic terms and holidays. We have moments of focus and attention, of flow and 'optimal experience' and performance; and then down time, preparation time, where the rhythm shifts. In examining a variety of performance groups – creative, artistic, musical and athletic teams, in 'Groups That Work' Hackman and colleagues comment on the rhythm of performance teams: each performance has its own rhythm, according to its purpose: practices and rehearsals start out low key, gradually building up in energy and tension until 'opening night'. For these performance teams, the play is their work, and their rhythm is matched in work away from traditionally creative industries. Hackman adds: 'temporal phenomena were everywhere' in the teams they studied, way beyond the creative sector. If a team can create a predictable rhythm for learning, it will become habit and those habits will enable the team to improve and sustain its performance.

What does a learning rhythm look like?

There are many opportunities that a team can take to develop a rhythm to its learning. Using the 10 Principles of Adaptable Teams (Chapter 3), alongside the team's own ground rules, we recommend looking at those opportunities, primarily alongside the operational conversations that are already being had. Those meetings can be made to work harder for the team if the team 'slows down to speed up'. Here are some ways in which clients have created their own team learning rhythm.

A. Team meetings

Check in (2 min. each)

- What has been the highlight for you in the last period?
- What have you really enjoyed away from work?
- What do you need to set aside to be focused on today's meeting?

Check out (1 min. each)

- What did you value about the meeting today?
- What one thing would you change about the meeting to improve it?

Slow down to speed up (SDTSU) moments (10 min. total)

- What are you noticing about how the team is working today?
- What changes do you think we need to make?

(This can be one person who shares their observations, all team members or simply those who wish to speak.)

B. One-to-ones (leader/team member)

Less frequent

- Ask them to prepare their scoring on the 'results' model (Chapter 8 on 'Results') and discuss them, concluding with an action conversation.

More frequent

- What challenges are you grappling with?
- What support do you need and from whom in the team?
- What requests do you have for me?

Or an alternative . . .

- What do you notice about your performance in the team?
- What is going well for you in the team?
- What might you change?
- What resources/skills could you bring that you are holding back on?
- What changes can we make in the team to improve our capacity to deliver?

C. One-to-ones in a structured team learning session

We use a device called 'tell me' (Downey 2014) with prompts for a paired conversation within workshops. You can create your own, of course, and it is useful for the questions to become increasingly challenging or focus on specific aspects of team functioning or task progress. Here are some of the kinds of prompts we use:

Tell me . . .

- Something this team is addressing well
- Something that this team is not confronting that it needs to
- A goal this team has that is in jeopardy
- A goal that this team has in which it will excel
- A niggle that you have had with me over the last period
- A niggle you think I might have had with you over the last period
- An outstanding ability of yours
- How you can use that in service of this team.

Scrums, sprints, stand-ups and retrospectives

Along with the continuous improvement approaches of Lean, Agile and the like, come meeting structures that create a work programme 'rhythm' that organize work, keep the team focused on the section of activity they are in and give time for reflection. Adjusting these to suit your own purposes as an organization and as a team is a great opportunity. I have clients who use the Lean Visual Management Board process and with the team standing at the board regularly, everyone gets a chance to reflect and refocus on the metrics that matter and the activities that will make a difference. Even a simple Kanban board used weekly to move tasks through the headings of to do/doing/done can invoke a useful team rhythm – there does, however, need to be attention to the learning process, beyond the operational one. Exploring and adapting these approaches and making them your own could allow your team to ensure it is genuinely anticipating and adapting to the context, to stakeholders and the system it serves.

D. Quarterly off-sites

Many teams we work with set aside a day or two every quarter to perform a deep dive and to reconnect as a team – and for distributed teams this can still be achieved remotely. The subject matter may be the team itself, or it may be particular challenges that the team is facing. Space is always afforded, however, to understand how the team is working, and what needs to change in order that it can stay on track or improve its results.

There are a number of ways of stimulating conversation over and above the tools and techniques shared in previous chapters.

A series of questions within these away-days may look like this:

- What are you noticing about stakeholders?
- What are you noticing about the team and its dynamic?
- What results are we getting (use the results model to stimulate debate)?
- What story would you tell if someone asked you about the events of the last quarter?
- What did we achieve in the last quarter?
- What specifically did we do together to achieve those results?
- What have we learnt about the team and our task that will assist us in the next phase?
- What else do we need to do in order to be able to continue to improve our result(s)?

Time

Time and how we use it; do we have time for this?

Daniel Kahneman, the psychologist and economist, won the Nobel Prize in 2002 for his work that distinguishes two different kinds of thinking – 'system one' and 'system two' – thinking fast and thinking slow. Both types of thinking are available, yet sometimes we choose the wrong type. Thinking that is fastest is automatic, intuitive, draws on previous learning – and in procedural tasks that repeat, that's very helpful. However, if one switches to tasks that require a bit more thought or awareness where not all the same conditions apply, despite the fact that the task may look the same as one you have done before, slow thinking is required. Turning your car into moving traffic, for instance, is a 'system two' activity – this stops your conversation and usefully so, realizing you cannot do other things at the same time. Kahneman (2011) says that we can concentrate, but mostly we avoid it because it can be demanding. Intelligent people, in particular, who can solve problems easily can get away with being more lazy.

This is the root of our principle 'slow down to speed up'. If one is operating at great speed, it is difficult to harvest the learning as you go and easier to regress to automatic thinking when the task requires something a different kind of thinking from you. As Kahneman himself points out, 'we can run or we can walk, we have a choice'. And all choices have consequences.

The challenge that many teams face is setting aside time to learn from each other and from their own experiences in context, and to do so in such a way that it enhances team capability. While many teams may have an operational rhythm, this may only pay lip service to the learning process, which is left fundamentally down to individuals in the team. And yet, of course, team learning is a team sport – it's difficult to do it alone. Indeed, as we have examined, the team dynamic and the team's sense of itself is a movable feast and learning how to keep it moving in the right direction again is a team endeavour.

Since we are recommending a team learning rhythm, it's useful to consider different ways of looking at the time that we do have. One distinction that is perhaps useful is between clock time, which is objective and measurable, and subjective time, which depends upon what one is doing, one's personal sense of time passing (which is rooted in one's past and current beliefs), and one's psychological state. The Greeks made a distinction between these two types of time, calling the first Chronos and the second Kairos. As human beings we have an internal clock, a sense of time seated in our brain. It runs just over a 24-hour period and is subject to influence by light and dark. This is why shift workers and those who travel between time zones can find themselves and their bodies disorientated and needing to apply remedy to get themselves back on track. When one has a serious illness that may be life-threatening, or encounters bereavement, our experience of time passing changes, and we may begin to use our time differently (Zimbardo 2008).

How a team can see time differently: framing time differently

In her book *Teaming*, Amy Edmondson (2012) makes an important distinction between teams that organize to learn and teams that don't. The important ingredient in teams who are organized to learn is 'framing'. A frame is, as we have been describing earlier, based on beliefs and assumptions. We look at everything through a set of beliefs and assumptions and that causes us to act in certain ways. Edmondson makes a distinction between a frame that is helpful for the team to learn and one that is less helpful.

If one frames the situation as a 'performance situation', one is going to be more risk averse and less willing to persist through obstacles than when we embark on the same task and see it as a 'learning situation'. In addition, if one has a 'promotion orientation' when one is approaching a task we focus on ideals, goals and an eagerness to attain them – we are seeking to gain something. This is in contrast to a 'prevention orientation' when approaching a task – where one looks at that task with a sense of obligation and vigilance against loss, where new situations are 'opportunities to lose ground'.

Edmondson (2019) proposes three critical dimensions for successful framing that made a difference in her study of cardiac teams implementing a new cardiac procedure:

- **The leader's role:** Whether the surgeon, as the team leader, framed himself as an 'interdependent team member' or an 'individual expert'
- **The team's role:** Whether the team role was framed as empowered partners or skilled support staff
- **Project purpose:** Whether the project purpose was communicated as 'aspirational' or 'defensive'.

A final distinction in framing: this framing was an important consideration in contributing to a team choosing to learn and has a mindset that Edmondson labels 'action as learning'. If one sees 'action as efficiency', there is implicitly less opportunity to learn, more direction from the top and less engagement from those doing the work. The more the team sees its work as 'action as learning', the more chance there will be to learn from its experiences.

Teams and flow

From team learning rhythm to teams in flow

In 1992, I took a plane from London Heathrow to Chicago O'Hare Airport to spend time with my brother. At the airport bookshop I bought a book called *Flow – The Psychology of Optimal Experience* (Csikszentmihalyi 2002; it has since changed its title to *Flow: The Psychology of Happiness*). It's one of the few books that I've read cover to cover pretty much in one sitting. Csikszentmihalyi had emigrated to America from Hungary aged 22 and had been studying the psychology of optimal experience in an innovative way at the University of Chicago for some time. His wide-reaching book seems to cover every aspect of human experience from work through to leisure, sex and sport, and provides a template by which we could all explore our own huge potential.

Definition of flow

Flow is an 'optimal experience' in which one is completely engaged in a task that is demanding of our skill. We are applying ourselves so completely in the moment that distractions fall away, and focus is absolute. It is in these moments that we are free to both learn from immediate feedback and apply that learning to create superior performance. We have all had these moments of complete absorption and self-forgetfulness, and these are often when we report having performed beyond our own expectations of ourselves.

If we want to create an experience of flow, then there are a number of characteristics of that experience that are relatively straightforward to create. They are as follows:

1 Embark on a **challenging** activity that requires sufficient **skill**.
2 Set clear **goals** for each element.
3 Get immediate **feedback** on your actions.
4 **Lose yourself** (your self-consciousness) in the task.
5 **Concentrate and focus** to the exclusion of distractions (interferences).
6 **Notice** what is happening (non-judgementally).
7 **Let go** of any fear of failure.
8 **Raise the stakes** if the activity becomes boring.

(Adapted from *Flow: The Psychology of Optimal Experience* by M. Csikszentmihalyi.)

This applies to individuals as well as to teams, in my experience. We can all tell sports teams that are 'over-thinking' in their play together. The team becomes self-conscious and hampered, apparently by its own brilliance. Ironically, in that process they look stupid, fumbling, inept. In contrast, other teams make it look easy; they have a sixth sense and seem to work so much more fluently together, learning as they go without effort.

The same is true of teams at work. Very often, not much divides great teams from mediocre ones – doing the simple things well is a huge contributor to 'playing a great game' as an executive team. As soon as the team gets self-conscious and begins to doubt itself, everything starts to unravel. Therefore, the more a team can spot opportunities for engagement in their activities collectively as opportunities for a flow state to be engendered, the more they will be able to not just enjoy their work in retrospect but also deliver their best work over time and be able to sustain it through their learning together.

As Csikszentmihalyi (2002) puts it:

> it is the full involvement of flow, rather than happiness that makes for excellence in life. When we are in flow, we are not happy, because to experience happiness we must focus on our inner states, and that would take attention away from the task at hand. If a rock climber takes time out to feel happy while negotiating a difficult move, he might fall to the bottom of the mountain. The surgeon can't afford to feel happy during a demanding operation . . . only after the task is completed do we have the leisure to look back on what has happened and then we are flooded with gratitude for the excellence of that experience – then in retrospect, we are happy. The happiness that follows flow is of our own making, and it leads to increasing complexity and growth in consciousness.

Once teams establish a rhythm and it becomes a set of team habits that are working well for the team, the team may begin to experience flow in its activities. There is less effort required to stay on track, less effort to switch from conversations about task to those about team dynamics and back again. Combining learning with operational conversations is therefore invaluable.

One such process is how some organizations are building into each project 'after action reviews' (taken from the US military) or 'retrospectives' (which are part of the 'agile' language and process). The purpose of these sessions is for a team to look back at a specific section of their work – a client pitch, an initiative, an improvement project, the last quarter, or even a specific event. The time is focused, say 60 minutes, includes all members of the team, and each prepares with set questions prior to the session.

The process may look like this:

1 Confirm principles/rules
2 Work these questions
  - What went well?
  - What would we change?
    o in what we did
    o in how we worked together
3 What will we do now and for next time?

What is crucial in all of these conversations is that there is sufficient psychological safety in the team and there is a focus on describing what happened, rather than calling out colleagues or blaming any failures on team members or context.

Learning organization

Connecting teams

Within the Adaptable Team approach is the proposition that leadership resides in each individual. The same is true of teams. Teams that can influence and connect with other teams across the organization are teams that are leading the organization – irrespective of their positional authority. The more organizations can establish that team-to-team network, where teams genuinely do engage and enrol each other, the more the organization becomes a learning organization and one as a whole that can deliver sustainable performance.

Whole systems learning

The learning organization

The modern learning organization is characterized by a growth mindset – one in which the basic assumption is that the opportunities to learn and develop are always there and the organization is also adapting to its environment. In a sense, what we are recommending here is that the organization as a whole engages with the learning process, just as different members of the team are encouraged to do so. The principal vehicle through which this can be done is Learning Summits.

Learning Summits

Once the team has established a team learning rhythm, has built confidence in its ability to deliver and is making progress, it may be important for the team's tasks, as well as for the organization more broadly, for that team to connect with others across the organization. It may even be mission-critical before this point, and part of the team's plan to be able to deliver its results.

The most useful way of connecting parts of the organizational system is with Learning Summits.

So, the purpose of Learning Summits may be as follows:

- For the team itself to enrol its own people in plans, initiatives, key changes and actions
- For the team to initiate and lead a shift in the wider system
- For the organization to harvest learning from its different parts
- For the organization to shift patterns and habits as part of an ongoing organizational development process or specific change initiative.

The benefits of Learning Summits

With careful crafting and the right teams in the room, the parts of the system begin to be connected and conversations about tasks and systems dynamics can be had live, and decisions made on the day about how to continue to improve. Often, this is the first time all the parts of the system will have been in the same room, so there is an opportunity to build relationships and establish trust as well as psychological safety. It becomes a public declaration of a change and with agreed actions and methodical follow-up, can create an enabling environment in which team learning begins to nurture a learning organization where the whole organization is learning from its experience and connecting the parts of the operation to learn and act together more effectively.

Learning Summits can involve anything from 15 to 150 people or more. They can bring together two teams or many more teams and groupings from the organization. As a team coach, ensuring the leaders of the different parts of the systems are involved early on is crucial, as is making sure the event has momentum, and practicality too. Learning Summits can become regular events and the organization can use the space they create to harvest learning and re-enforce connections and relationships, which enable better and more co-ordinated actions and better and more sustainable results.

Vignette: We worked with the project leadership team of 15 people in an oil and gas major that was charged with delivering a fully functioning plant in the

Middle East with a total of investment of around \$16 billion. Before they deployed in country, much of their work was in the UK with a distributed team from a variety of different parts of the business. After three workshops with the leadership team where we worked alongside the leader in grounding relationships and agreeing ways of working and engaging the goal sets, we suggested bringing all of the parties from around the business into one room to have a whole systems conversation. This had not been done before, though neither had this scale of project. So, in a huge ballroom in a hotel near London Heathrow, we brought all of the different parts of the system together – in total nearly one hundred people – and invited them for a day where they could engage with each other. It gave the leadership team the opportunity to set the tone for their work together in the next phase, and it allowed this multidisciplinary system to build relationships one discipline to another and agree how they were going to work together as well as give different groups feedback. The process needed quite a bit of detailed thinking to ensure chaos was avoided. The outcome was an engaged wider system and relationships that would endure, even when geographical dispersion for different stages of the project occurred.

Team working across organizational boundaries

The three most common organizational boundaries are: geographic (distance), knowledge, and status (Edmondson 2019). All of these can be attended to in physical or virtual Learning Summits. The most common challenge many clients face is the desire to break down 'silos' and create better connections between the parts of the organization, encouraging more cross boundary working. Learning Summits are a golden opportunity to meet that challenge.

For each of the categories of boundaries, Edmondson recommends the following: ensuring that there is a super-ordinate goal in the organization that appeals to all parties; the fostering of curiosity as to what is happening and what can be gained from engaging with other parts of the organization; and ensuring that there are good processes available for the cross team reworking and leadership that encourages such activity explicitly. She has additional tips, again, which can all be attended to with a pattern of effective Learning Summits.

- **To overcome geographic boundaries:** Encourage engagement with different parts of the organization and different teams, learning about local knowledge and expertise.
- **To overcome status boundaries:** Encourage the sharing of individual and personal perspectives, encouraging a collective identity rather than an individual or just team identity.
- **To overcome knowledge boundaries:** Encourage the sharing of expertise, and involvement in problem-solving through multidisciplinary groups, establishing a collective identity over individual teams (Edmondson 2019).

Vignette: 'Results Focus' was a programme that was initiated following external consultancy, Strategy Inc.'s, corporate wide assessment of what Energy plc needed to do to deliver on its ambitions. The role of performance coaching had become important, so a workshop for the top 40 leaders in the operation was designed to facilitate the change process and re-enforce the connection with a performance coaching approach. This was an explicit part of Strategy Inc.'s recommendations. The one-day session focused on the assumptions and principles that needed to be in place in order for behaviour to be consistent with the change the business aspired to. It then looked at 'rackets' (see Chapter 3) to understand where their behaviour was running counter to their commitments. These challenging conversations resulted in refreshed commitment behind Results Focus as well as the development of new commitments and shifted assumptions for day-to-day leadership.

Summary

- The ability of a team to learn is central to its ability to sustain performance over time.
- There are three levels of learning: Level 1 learning (the most transactional) is at its simplest about learning to improve our actions; Level 2 learning (dynamic learning) is about learning to reframe our thinking; Level 3 learning (the most transformational) is about how we experience ourselves and our identity, our purpose and learning to transform our leadership role.
- A team learning rhythm, often embedded alongside the team's operational rhythm, is a powerful way to ensure the team continues to learn as it works.
- Choosing to invest time in learning is an important step forward for the team. It helps the team 'slow down to speed up'. Looking differently at the time you invest is useful.
- The team can experience learning and performing to its peak when it is in flow.
- When a number of teams gather together to create an organizational learning rhythm in a Learning Summit, the organization can be transformed into a learning organization. This is one that 'is continually expanding its capacity to create its future' (Senge 1990).
- Learning organizations have as their basis a whole system learning approach that can help the organization to truly thrive.

Bibliography

Allen, N.J. and Hecht, T.D. (2004) The 'Romance of Teams': Toward an understanding of its psychological underpinnings and implications. *Journal of Occupational and Organizational Psychology*, 77: 439–461.

Amason, A.C. (1996) Distinguishing the effects of functional and dysfunctional conflict on strategic decision making: Resolving a paradox for top management teams. *The Academy of Management Journal*, 39: 123–148.

Argyris, C. (1991) Teaching smart people how to learn. *Harvard Business Review*, 4(2): 4–15.

Aube, C. and Rousseau, V. (2005) Team goal commitment and team effectiveness: The role of task interdependence and supportive behaviours. *Group Dynamics: Theory, Research and Practice*, 9(3): 189–204.

Bales, R.F. and Strodtbeck, F.L. (1951) Phases in group problem solving. *Journal of Abnormal and Social Psychology*, 46: 485–495.

Bandura, A. (1989) Self-regulation of motivation and action through internal standards and goal systems. In L.A. Pervin (Ed.) *Goal Concepts in Personality and Social Psychology* (pp. 19–85). Hillsdale, NJ: Erlbaum.

Bandura, A. (1997) *Self-efficacy: The Exercise of Control*. New York: Freeman.

Bandura, A. and Cervone, D. (1983) Self-evaluative and self-efficacy mechanisms governing the motivational effects of goal systems. *Journal of Personality and Social Psychology*, 45: 1017–1028.

Bartlett, C. and Ghoshal, S. (1991) Global strategic management: Impact on the new frontiers of strategy research. *Strategic Management Journal*, 12: 5–16.

Baumeister, R.F. and Leary, M.R. (1995) The need to belong: Desire for interpersonal attachments as a fundamental human motivation. *Psychological Bulletin*, 117: 497–529.

Bazigos, M. and Harter, J. (2016) Revisiting the matrix organisation. *McKinsey Quarterly*.

Beck, U.C. (2012) *Psychodynamic Coaching: Focus and Depth*. London: Karnac Books.

Bendersky, C. and Hays, N.A. (2012) Status conflict in groups. *Organization Science*, 23(2): 323–340.

Bennis W.G. (1951) *One Becoming a Leader*. Createspace Independent Publisher.

Bennis, W.G. and Shepard H.A. (1956) A theory of group development. *Human Relations*, 9: 415–435.

Bion, W.R. (1948) *Experiences in Groups*. London: Tavistock Publications.

Biswas-Diener, R. and Dean, B. (2010) *Positive Psychology Coaching, Putting the Science of Happiness to Work for Your Clients*. Hoboken, NJ: Wiley.

Block, P. (2011) *Flawless Consulting*. San Francisco, CA: Pfeiffer.

Bluckert, P. (2015) *Gestalt Coaching Right Here, Right Now*. London: McGraw-Hill.

Bohm, D. (1996) *On Dialogue* (edited by L. Nichol). New York: Psychology Press.

Braaten, L.J. (1974) Developmental phases of encounter groups and related intensive groups: A critical review of models and a new proposal. *Interpersonal Development*, 5: 112–129.

Brassey, J. and Kruyt, M. (2020) How to demonstrate calm and optimism in a crisis. *McKinsey Quarterly*.

Bratton, J. and Gold, J. (2012) *Human Resource Management: Theory and Practice* (5th edition). London: Palgrave.

Brown, T.C. and Latham, E.A. (n.d.) The effects of training in verbal self-guidance and goal setting on team playing behaviour. Paper presented at the meetings of the Academy of Management, Toronto, Canada.

Burnes, B. (2004) *Managing Change*. Harlow: Pearson.

Byan, J. and Locke, E.A. (1967) Goal setting as a means of increasing motivation. *Journal of Applied Psychology*, 51: 274–277.

Chang, A., Bordia, P. and Duck, P.B. (2003) Punctuated equilibrium and linear progression: Towards a new understanding of group development. *Academy of Management Journal*, 46(1): 106–117.

Chell, E. (2004) Critical incident technique. In C. Cassell and G. Symon (Eds.) *Essential Guide to Qualitative Methods in Organisational Research*. Thousand Oaks, CA: Sage.

Chesney, A. and Locke, E. (1991) An examination of the relationship among goal difficulty, business strategies and performance on a complex simulation task. *Academy of Management Journal*, 34: 400–424.

Clutterbuck, D. (2012) *Coaching the Team at Work*. London: Nicholas Brearley.

Cohen, S.G. and Bailey D.E. (1997) What makes teams work: Group effectiveness research from the shop floor to the executive suite. *Journal of Management*, 23(3): 239–290.

Cook, J. and Wall, T. (1980) New work attitude measures of trust, organizational commitment and personal need non-fulfilment. *Journal of Occupational Psychology*, 53(1): 39–52.

Csikszentmihalyi, M. (2002) *Flow: The Psychology of Optimal Experience*. London: Random House,

De Board, R. (1978) *The Psychoanalysis of Organisations*. London: Tavistock Publications.

De Wit, F.R.C., Greer, L.L. and Jehn, K.A. (2012) The paradox of intragroup conflict: A meta-analysis. *Journal of Applied Psychology*, 97(2): 360–390.

Deloittes (2017) *Deloittes Human Capital Report*. https://www2.deloitte.com/content/dam/Deloitte/global/Documents/About-Deloitte/central-europe/ce-global-human-capital-trends.pdf

Dirks, K.T. (1999) The effects of interpersonal trust on workgroup performance. *Journal of Applied Psychology*, 84(3): 445–455.

Doerr, J. (2018) *Measure What Matters*. London: Penguin Random House.

Downey, M. (2014) *Effective Modern Coaching*. London: LID Publishing.

Drennan, D. (1992) *Transforming Company Culture*. London: McGraw-Hill.

Drucker, P. (1954) *The Practice of Management*. New York: Harper & Row.

Drucker, P. (1999) *Managing for Results*. Boston, MA: Harvard Business School Press.

Druskat, V. (2004) *Teams That Succeed*. Boston, MA: Harvard Business School Press.

Dweck, C. (2012) *Mindset: Changing the Way You Think to Fulfil Your Potential*. London: Robinson.

Eden, D. (1985) A true field experiment at three levels of rigor. *Journal of Applied Psychology*, 70(1): 94–100.

Edmondson, A. (2012) *Teaming*. Boston, MA: Harvard Business School Press.

Edmondson, A. (2019) *The Fearless Organization*. Hoboken, NJ: Wiley.

Egan, G. (2017) *The Skilled Helper*. Pacific Grove, CA: Brooks/Cole.

Eldredge, N. and Gould, S.J. (1972) Punctuated equilibria: An alternative to phyletic gradualism. In T.J. Schopf (Ed.) *Models in Paleobiology* (pp. 82–115). San Francisco, CA: Freeman, Cooper and Co.

Fay, D., Borrill, C., Amir, Z., Haward, R. and West, M. (2010) Getting the most out of multidisciplinary teams: A multi-sample study of team innovation in health care. *Journal of Occupational and Organizational Psychology*, 79(4): 553–567.

Ferenczi, S. (1916) *Contributions to Psychoanalysis*. Boston, MA: Richard Badiger.

Flanagan, J.C. (1954) The critical incident. *Psychological Bulletin*, 51(4): 327–358.

Forsyth, D.R. (2014) *Group Dynamics* (6th edition). Belmont, CA: Wadsworth Cengage Learning.

Frankl, V. (2004) *Man's Search for Meaning*. London: Random House.

Fredrickson, B.L. (2004) The broaden and build theory of positive emotions. Paper to the Royal Society, published online.

Freud, S. (1922) *Group Psychology and the Analysis of the Ego*. International Psychoanalytic Press. UK: Empire Books.

Gallup (2019) Employees need high wellbeing for high performance, *Gallup Workplace*. Available at: https://www.gallup.com/workplace/215924/well-being.aspx

Gersick, C.J.G. (1988) Time and transition in work teams: Towards a new model of group development. *Academy of Management Journal*, 31: 9–41.

Gersick, C.J.G. and Hackman, J.R. (1990) Habitual routines in task performing teams. *Organizational Behavior and Human Decision Processes*, 47: 65–97.

Glaser, B.G. and Strauss, A.L. (1967) *The Discovery of Grounded Theory: Strategies for Qualitative Research*. New York: Aldine.

Glassop, L. (2002) The organisational benefits of teams. *Human Relations*, 55(2): 225–249.

Goodwin, P. and Page, T. (2008) *From Hippos to Gazelles, How Leaders Create Leaders*. Chichester: Kingsham Press.

Gratton, L. (2007) *Hot Spots, Why Some Companies Buzz with Energy and Innovation and Others Don't*. London: Financial Times/Prentice-Hall.

Guzzo, R.A. and Dickson, M.W. (1996) Teams in organizations. *Annual Review of Psychology*, 47: 307–338.

Guzzo, R.A., Yost, P.R., Campbell, R.J. and Shea, G.P. (1993) Potency in groups: Articulating a construct. *British Journal of Social Psychology*, 32: 87–106.

Guzzo, R., Salas, E. and Associates (1995) *Team Effectiveness and Decision-making in Organizations*. San Francisco, CA: Jossey-Bass.

Hackman, J.R. (1987) The design of work teams. In J.W. Lorsch (Ed.) *Handbook of Organisational Behaviour* (pp. 315–342). Englewood Cliffs, NJ: Prentice-Hall.

Hackman, J.R. (Ed.) (1990) *Groups That Work (and Those That Don't)*. San Francisco, CA: Jossey-Bass.

Hackman, J.R. (2002) *Leading Teams, Setting the Stage for Great Performances*. Boston, MA: Harvard Business School Press.

Hackman, J.R. and Wageman R. (2005) A theory of team coaching. *Academy of Management Review*, 30: 269–287.

Hammond, C. (2007) Impacts of lifelong learning upon emotional resilience, psychological and mental health: Fieldwork evidence. *Oxford Review of Education*, 30(4): 551–568.

Harrison, R. (1971) Role negotiation: A tough minded approach to team development. In W. Burke and H.A. Hornstein (Eds.) *The Social Technology of Organization Development* (pp. 84-96). Fairfax, VA: NTL Learning Resources.

Harter, J. (March 2020) What employees need from leadership right now. https://www.gallup.com/workplace/297497/covid-employees-need-leaders-right.aspx

Hartley, J. (2004) Case study research. In C. Cassel and G. Symon (Eds.) *Essential Guide to Qualitative Methods in Organizational Research*. London: Sage.

Hatfield, E., Cacioppo, J.T. and Rapson, R.L. (1993) Emotional contagion. *Current Directions in Psychological Science*, 2(3): 96–99.

Hawkins, P. (2011) *Leadership Team Coaching. Developing Collective Transformational Leadership*. London: Kogan Page.

Hawkins, P. and Smith, N. (2013) *Coaching, Mentoring and Organizational Consultancy, Supervision and Development*. Maidenhead: Open University Press.

Heron, J. (1999) *The Complete Facilitator's Handbook*. London: Kogan Page.

Heron, J. (2001) *Helping the Client*. London: Kogan Page.

Janis, I.L. (1972) *Victims of Teamthink*. Boston, MA: Houghton Mifflin.

Janis, I. (1991) Groupthink. In E. Griffin (Ed.) *A First Look at Communication Theory* (pp. 235–246). New York: McGraw-Hill.

Jarvenpaa, S.L. and Leidner, D.E. (1999) Communication and trust in global virtual teams. *Organization Science*, 10(6): 791–815.

Jehn, K.A. (1995) A multimethod examination of the benefits and detriments of intra-group conflict. *Administrative Science Quarterly*, 40(2): 256–282.

Jones, R., Napiersky, U. and Lyubovnikova, J. (2019) Conceptualizing the distinctiveness of team coaching. *Journal of Managerial Psychology*, 34(2): 62–78.

Kahneman, D. (2011) *Thinking Fast and Slow*. London: Penguin.

Kandola, B. (2009) *The Value of Difference*. Oxford: Pearn Kandola.

Kantor, D. (2012) *Reading the Room: Group Dynamics for Coaches and Leaders*. San Francisco, CA: Jossey-Bass.

Katzenbach, J.R. and Smith, D.K. (1993) *The Wisdom of Teams*. Boston, MA: Harvard Business School Press.

Katzenbach, J.R. and Smith, D.K. (2001) *The Discipline of Teams*. Boston, MA: Harvard Business School Press.

Kayes, C.D. (2004) The 1996 Mount Everest climbing disaster: The breakdown of learning in teams. *Human Relations*, 57(10): 1263–1284.

Kets de Vries, M.F.R. (2012) The group coaching conundrum. INSEAD Faculty and Research Working Paper 2012/53/EFE. Fontainebleau: INSEAD.

Kilmann, R.H. and Thomas, K.W. (1977) Developing a forced-choice measure of conflict-handling behavior: The 'MODE' instrument. *Educational and Psychological Measurement*, 37(2): 309–325.

Knights, D. and McCabe, D. (2000) Bewitched, bothered and bewildered: The meaning and experience of team working for employees in an automobile company. *Human Relations*, 53(11): 1481–1517.

Kramer, R.M. and Tyler, T.R. (1996) *Trust in Organisations*. London: Sage.

Kubler-Ross, E. and Kessler, D. (2014) *On Grief and Grieving: Finding the Meaning of Grief Through the Five Stages*. London: Simon & Schuster.

Lacoursiere, R.A. (1974) A group method to facilitate learning during the stages of psychiatric affiliation. *International Journal of Group Psychotherapy*, 24: 342–351.

Lansisalmi, H., Peiro, J.M. and Kivimaki, M. (2004) Grounded theory in organisational research. In C. Cassell and G. Symon (Eds.) *Essential Guide to Qualitative Methods in Organisational Research*. London: Sage.

Latham, G.P. and Kinne, S.B. (1974) Improving job performance through training in goal setting. *Journal of Applied Psychology*, 59(2): 187–191.

Latham, G.P. and Locke E.A. (1975) Increasing productivity with decreasing time limits: A field replication of Parkinson's Law. *Journal of Applied Psychology*, 60(4): 524–526.

Latham, G.P. and Seijts, G.H. (1999) The effects of proximal and distal goals on performance of a moderately complex task. *Journal of Applied Psychology*, 20(4): 421–429.

Lawrence, P.R. and Lorsch, J.W. (1967) *Organization and Environment*. Boston, MA: Harvard Business School, Division of Research. (Reissued as a Harvard Business School Classic, Harvard Business School Press, 1986.)

Leary-Joyce, J. and Lines, H. (2018) *Systemic Team Coaching*. St Albans: AoEC Press.

Lencioni, P. (2005) *Overcoming the Five Dysfunctions of a Team*. San Francisco, CA: Jossey-Bass.

Lencioni, P. (2011) *The Five Dysfunctions of a Team*. San Francisco, CA: Jossey-Bass.

Lerner, J.S. and Tetlock, P.E. (1999) Accounting for the effects of accountability. *Psychological Bulletin*, 125(2): 255–275.

Lewin, K. (1947) Frontiers in group dynamics. *Human Relations*, 1(1): 143–153.

Lewin, K. (1951) *Field Theory in Social Science: Selected Theoretical Papers* (edited by D. Cartwright). New York: Harper & Brothers.

Lewis, P.J. and Tully, M.P. (2009) Uncomfortable prescribing decisions in hospitals: The impact of teamwork. *Journal of the Royal Society of Medicine*, 102(11): 481–488.

LinkedIn (2018) *LinkedIn Workplace Learning Report.* https://learning.linkedin.com/resources/workplace-learning-report-2018

Lipnack, J. and Stamps, J. (2000) *Virtual Teams: People Working Across Boundaries with Technology.* New York: Wiley.

Locke, E.A. and Bryan, J. (1969) The directing functions of goals in task performance. *Organizational Behavior and Human Performance*, 4: 35–42.

Locke, E.A. and Latham, G.P. (2002) Building a practically useful theory of goal setting and task motivation: A 35-year odyssey. *American Psychologist*, 57(9): 707–717.

Long, S. (2012) *Transforming Experience in Organisations: A Framework for Organisational Research and Consultancy.* Abingdon: Routledge.

Macy, B.A. and Izumi, H. (1993) *Organizational Change, Design and Work Innovation: A Meta-analysis of 131 North American Field Studies – 1961–1991. Research in Organizational Change and Design* (Vol. 7). Greenwich, CT: JAI Press.

Marks, A., Mathieu, J.E. and Zaccaro, S.J. (2001) A temporally based framework and taxonomy of team processes. *Academy of Management Review*, 26(3): 356–376.

McAllister, D.J. (1995) Affect- and cognition-based trust as foundations for interpersonal cooperation in organizations. *Academy of Management Journal*, 38(1): 24–59.

McGrath, J.E. (1984) *Groups: Interaction and Performance.* Englewood Cliffs, NJ: Prentice-Hall.

Meuller, F., Proctor, S. and Buchanan, D. (2000) Team working in its context: Antecedents, nature and dimensions. *Human Relations*, 53: 1387–1423.

Mitleton-Kelly, E. (2003) Ten principles of complexity and enabling infrastructures. In E. Mitleton-Kelly (Ed.) *Complex Systems and Evolutionary Perspectives of Organisations: The Application of Complexity Theory to Organisations* (pp. 23–50). Oxford: Elsevier.

Mohammed, S. and Angell, L.C. (2004) Surface- and deep-level diversity in workgroups: Examining the moderating effects of team orientation and team process on relationship conflict. *Journal of Organisational Behaviour*, 25(8): 1015–1039.

Mor Barak, M.E., Cherin, D.A. and Berkman, S. (1998) Organizational and personal dimensions in diversity climate: Ethnic and gender differences in employee perceptions. *Journal of Applied Behavioral Science*, 34(1): 82–104. https://doi.org/10.1177/0021886398341006

Nembhard, I.M. and Edmondson, A.C. (2006) Making it safe: The effects of leader inclusiveness and professional status on psychological safety and improvement efforts in health care teams. *Journal of Organizational Behavior*, 27(7): 941–966.

Patterson, K., Grenny, J., McMillan, R. and Switzler, A. (2011) *Crucial Conversations.* London: McGraw-Hill.

Pearson, C.A.L. (1992) Autonomous workgroups: An evaluation at an industrial site. *Human Relations*, 45(9): 905–936.

Pedde, J. (2018) *Orchestrating Change – How to Navigate Complexity and Get Results.* Victoria, BC: Tellwell Talent.

Personnel Today (19 December 2017) Could technology help to reduce conflict at work? https://www.personneltoday.com/hr/technology-help-reduce-conflict-work/

Peterson, C., Park, N. and Sweeney, P.J. (2008) Group well-being: Morale from a positive psychology perspective. *Applied Psychology: An International Review*, 57(s1): 19–36.

Pidgeon, N. and Henwood, K. (1997) Using grounded theory in psychological research. In N. Hayes (Ed.) *Doing Qualitative Analysis in Psychology* (pp. 245–273). Hove: Psychology Press.

Pritchard, R.D., Jones, S.D., Roth, P.L., Stuebing, K.K. and Ekeberg, S.E. (1988) Effects of group feedback, goal setting, and incentives on organizational productivity. *Journal of Applied Psychology*, 73(2): 337–358.

Robinson, S.L. (1996) Trust and breach of the psychological contract. *Administrative Science Quarterly*, 41(4): 574–599.

Runkel, P.J., Lawrence, M., Oldfield, S., Rider, M. and Clark, C. (1971) Stages of group development: An empirical test of Tuckman's hypothesis. *Journal of Applied Behavioural Science*, 7(2): 180–193.

Ryan, T.A. (1970) *Intentional Behaviour*. New York: Ronald Press.

Salas, E., Ricoh, R. and Passmore, J. (2005) *The Psychology of Team Working and Collaborative Processes*. London: Wiley Blackwell.

Schein, E.H. (1999) *Process Consultation Revisited: Building the Helping Relationship*. London: Prentice-Hall.

Schein, E.H. (2015) *Helping: How to Offer, Give, and Receive Help*. San Francisco, CA: Berrett-Koehler Publishers.

Schutz, W. (1994) *The Human Element*. San Francisco, CA: Jossey-Bass.

Scott Peck, M. (1990) *A Different Drum*. London: Arrow Books.

Seijts, G.H. and Latham, G.P. (2000) The effects of goal setting and group size on performance in a social dilemma. *Canadian Journal of Behavioural Science / Revue canadienne des sciences du comportement*, 32(2): 104–116.

Seligman, M. (2011) *Flourishing: A New Understanding of Happiness and Wellbeing*. London: Nicholas Brealey.

Seligman, M. (2017) *Authentic Happiness*. New York: Simon & Schuster.

Senge, P.M. (1990) *The Fifth Discipline: The Art and Practice of the Learning Organization*. New York: Doubleday.

Senge, P., Kleiner, A., Roberts, C., Ross, R., Rogers, C. and Smith, B. (1994) *The Fifth Discipline Fieldbook: Strategies and Tools for Building a Learning Organization*. London: Nicholas Brealey Publishing.

Senge, P., Kleiner, A., Roberts, C., Ross, R., Roth, G. and Smith, B. (2014) *The Dance of Change*. Nottingham: Lifespace Publishing.

Shaw, D., Zhu, J. and Duffy, M.K. (2010) A contingency model of conflict and team effectiveness. *Journal of Applied Psychology*, 96(2): 391–400.

Smith, K.K., Simmons, V.M. and Thames, T.B. (1989) Fix the women: An intervention into an organizational conflict based on parallel process thinking. *Journal of Applied Behavioral Science*, 25(1): 11–29.

Spitz, H. and Sadock, B. (1973) Psychiatric training of graduate nursing students. *NY State Journal of Medicine*, 73(11): 1334–1338.

Stewart, G.L. (2006) A meta-analytic review of relationships between team design features and team performance. *Journal of Management*, 32(1): 29–55.

Stewart, I. and Joines, V. (2012) *TA Today*. Nottingham: Lifespace Publishing.

Sy, T., Côté, S. and Saavedra, R. (2005) The contagious leader: impact of the leader's mood on the mood of group members, group affective tone, and group processes. *Journal of Applied Psychology*, 90(2): 295–305.

Sy, T., Côté, S. and Van Kleef, G.A. (2013) The social effects of emotion regulation in organizations. In A.A. Grandey, J.M. Diefendorff and D.E. Rupp (Eds.) *Emotional Labor in the 21st Century: Diverse Perspectives on Emotion Regulation at Work* (pp. 79–100). New York: Routledge.

Syer, J. and Connolly, C. (1996) *How Teamwork Works, The Dynamics of Effective Team Development*. London: McGraw-Hill.

Tate, W. (2009) *The Search for Leadership: An Organisational Perspective*. London: Triarchy Press.

Thompson, L. (2007) *Making the Team: A Guide for Managers.* London: Pearson.

Thorndike, E.L. (1927) The law of effect. *American Journal of Psychology,* 39: 212–222.

Thornton, C. (2016) *Group and Team Coaching The Essential Guide.* London: Routledge.

Thurman, M.P. (1991) Strategic leadership. Presentation to the Strategic Leadership Conference, US Army War College, Carlisle Barracks, PA.

Trist, E.L. and Bamforth, K.W. (1951) Some social and psychological consequences of the longwall method of coal-getting. *Human Relations,* 4(1): 3–38.

Trist, E.L., Brown, G. and Susman, G. (1977) An experiment in autonomous working in an Australian coal mine. *Human Relations,* 30(3): 201–236.

Tuckman, B.W. (1965) Developmental sequence in small groups. *Psychological Bulletin,* 63(6): 384–399.

Tuckman, B.W. and Jensen, M.A.C. (1977) Stages of small-group development revisited. *Group and Organization Management,* 2(4): 419–427.

Turner, J.C., Brown, R.J. and Tajfelk, H. (1989) Social comparison and group interest in ingroup favouritism. *European Journal of Social Psychology,* 9(2): 187–204.

Van der Haar, D. and Hosking, D.M. (2004) Evaluating appreciative enquiry: A relational constructionist perspective. *Human Relations,* 57: 1017–1036.

Wageman, R. (1995) Interdependence and group effectiveness. *Administrative Science Quarterly,* 40: 145–180.

Wageman, R., Nunes, D., Burruss, J. and Hackman R. (2008) *Senior Leadership Teams.* Boston, MA: Harvard Business School Press.

Wall, T.D., Kemp, N.J., Jackson, P.R. and Clegg, C. (1986) Outcomes of autonomous work-groups: A long-term field experiment. *Academy of Management Journal,* 29(2): 280–304.

Wang, D., Zhang, Z. and Waldman, D. (2013) A meta-analysis of shared leadership and team effectiveness. *Journal of Applied Psychology,* 99(2): 181–198.

Watkins, J. and Mohr, B. (2001) *Appreciative Inquiry, Change at the Speed of Imagination.* San Francisco, CA: Jossey-Bass.

Weick, K.E. (1995) *Sensemaking in Organizations.* Thousand Oaks, CA: Sage.

West, M.A. (2012) *Effective Teamwork: Practical Lessons from Organizational Research* (3rd edition). Chichester: Wiley.

Whittington, J. (2012) *Systemic Coaching and Constellations – An Introduction to the Principles, Practices and Application.* London: Kogan Page.

Winters, D. and Latham, G. (1996) The effect of learning versus outcome goals on a simple versus a complex task. *Group and Organization Management,* 21: 236–250.

Wisner, P.S. and Feist H.A. (2001) Does teaming pay off? *Strategic Finance,* 82(8): 58–64.

Wood, R. and Locke, E. (1990) Goal setting and strategy effects on complex tasks. In B. Staw and L. Cummings (Eds.) *Research in Organization Behavior* (Vol. 12, pp. 73–109). Greewich, CT: JAI Press.

Yearta, S.K., Maitlis, S. and Briner, R.B. (1995) An exploratory study of goal setting in theory and practice: A motivational technique that works? *Journal of Occupational and Organizational Psychology,* 68(3): 237–252.

Yukl, G. (2019) *Leadership in Organizations.* London: Pearson.

Yukl, G.A. (2002) *Leadership in Organizations* (5th edition). Upper Saddle River, NJ: Prentice-Hall.

Zander, R.S. and Zander, B. (2000) *The Art of Possibility.* London: Penguin.

Zimbardo, P. (2008) *The Time Paradox – Using the New Psychology of Time to Your Advantage.* London: Random House.

Zurcher, L.A., Jr. (1969) Stages of development in property program neighborhood action committees. *Journal of Applied Behavioral Science,* 5(2): 223–258.

Index

Page numbers in italics are figures; with 't' are tables.